DOMINIK EBERHARD

The Network

CORNELSEN
ENGLISH
LIBRARY

Cornelsen

Cornelsen English Library
Dominik Eberhard · The Network

Verlagsredaktion
Kirsten Bleck, Jennifer O'Hagan

Umschlaggestaltung
hawemannundmosch, Konzeption und Gestaltung, Berlin

Titelbild
flydragon/Shutterstock

Illustration
Gabo, Berlin

Gestaltung & technische Umsetzung
Buchgestaltung+, Berlin

Passende Arbeitsblätter und weitere Hilfen zu diesem Titel gibt es unter:
www.cornelsen.de/cel

www.cornelsen.de

1. Auflage, 2. Druck 2014

Alle Drucke dieser Auflage sind inhaltlich unverändert und können im Unterricht nebeneinander verwendet werden.

Druck: Offizin Andersen Nexö Leipzig

ISBN 978-3-06-033218-2

Inhalt gedruckt auf säurefreiem Papier aus nachhaltiger Forstwirtschaft.

Contents

CHAPTER ONE A new friend

"Kevin wants to be your friend".

The short message suddenly popped up right in the middle of Jenny Anderson's *Network* profile.

"Who is this guy?" she thought and clicked on the link that, after about twenty seconds, directed her to Kevin's profile. She briefly looked at the three pictures that were like a visiting card to his *Network* profile.

"Oh no, he's the one that Vicky brought along to the cinema the other day!"

Jenny remembered the rather short, thin boy with glasses who joined them to see *Twilight* last Saturday. He didn't say much that evening, and the only time he spoke to Jenny was when he was introduced to her by Jenny's best friend, Vicky. Of course that was no big deal for Jenny since she did not fancy him at all. Now she was wondering what to do. She looked at Kevin's list of friends.

"Oh, what's that? He's friends with Alan," Jenny suddenly noticed. Alan Shearer was quite a popular boy from Jenny's parallel form. She had always found him interesting but had never dared to make a move.

"Can't do any harm, then," Jenny decided and clicked the OK button. About a minute later, a new pop-up message announced: "You are now friends with Kevin!" Jenny scrolled down the list that now contained 128 friends. "Not too bad," she thought.

She went back to her comments. In the middle of Jenny's *Network* profile was a section where she and everyone she had accepted as a friend could write messages and upload pictures, or even videos. Below these, people could comment on anything that had been posted.

"*Twilight* is brainless! What a boring film!" someone called Alex Lawson had written.

"Rubbish! It was great and exciting. Great acting. Good story. Go and see it everyone," Jenny typed into the line below the previous comment. She pressed 'Enter' and her comment appeared as a new entry on her profile.

Jenny scrolled down. There were twelve pictures of some teenagers at a party that Vicky had taken and uploaded. Several people had already commented: "Great party", "You look really drunk, Vicky", and "You should make a face like that more often! lol!" Then she saw that a new comment had been posted by a girl called Emily: "Oops! Jenny looks a bit chubby on that one, doesn't she?"

"Bitch!" Jenny said out loud. "Who does she think she is?" She got up from her chair, walked over to the other side of her small room and had a long look into the large mirror on the wall. She bent forward quite close to the mirror and examined her face. Her skin was smooth enough. She stepped back again and turned to the side. Then she lifted her T-shirt up a bit to look at her stomach.

"Perhaps she's right. It could be a bit flatter," Jenny said to herself. "I really should do more sport, or maybe eat less?"

She walked back to her computer and looked for a suitable picture of Emily to write a similar comment, but then she gave up on the idea. Instead, she scrolled up again and began to write a new message.

"Holidays are over, school starts tomorrow. Can't wait to see you all again, but I'm not too keen on classes. Wish we could have schools without teachers. They're just so annoying!"

At that moment, the door to her room suddenly opened and Jenny's mother walked in. She was forty years old, slim, and looking a bit stressed. Jenny turned around quickly.

"Mum! Could you please knock on the door before you come in? I've told you before!"

"Why? There's only you in here, isn't there? Anyway, have you finished getting ready for tomorrow? You promised to revise your French vocab. And just look at your room! When will you ever start tidying it up yourself without me having to tell you? Instead of surfing the internet all day and night!"

Jenny kept her eyes on the screen while her mother was talking to her and getting more and more excited.

"Are you still on *The Network*? I can't believe it. If you ask me, that thing should be banned. It's addictive!"

Jenny turned around slowly and looked at her mother.

"Mum, can't you just leave me in peace? There's nothing wrong with *The Network* – this is how people keep in touch today. Don't be so old-fashioned! The only thing in this room that should be banned is this stupid old computer that takes ages to load a website or download a file. I'm glad my friends can't see this old rubbish! It's bad enough I've only got this really old mobile phone! I know they make fun of it behind my back! Even Vicky has got a smartphone!"

Mrs Anderson's face went red.

"All right. Things aren't good enough any more for our young lady? Our young lady is used to a higher standard of living? Perhaps her mother should work a bit harder so our young lady can buy the latest technical equipment?"

"Mum, I didn't say that!"

"Perhaps the next thing our young lady wants is to live in Kensington and not in Wood Green in North London!"

"Come on, Mum, that's ridiculous!"

"Listen, it wasn't my choice to be stuck in a shabby place like this with a shabby job. If your father hadn't run off with another woman, we would be a happy family that could live a normal life like everybody else."

"I know, Mum. You've told me before."

Mrs Anderson's eyes filled with tears.

"Darling, I just worry about you. I'm worried about your GCSEs. You want to go to university. You want to get a good job and have a better life than this."

Without another word, Mrs Anderson left the room, sobbing quietly.

Jenny took a deep breath and stared at her computer screen. Her last comment about her teachers was still there: "They're just so annoying!" She took the keyboard and slowly added: "Just like my mum!" Then she pressed 'Enter' and sighed.

It felt as if this time the 'Enter' key had a different function because suddenly a window popped up.

"Kevin wants to invite you to a chat".

"This guy is really quick," Jenny thought.

She didn't know what to do. Why did he seem so keen now when he hadn't said a single word last Saturday? The two buttons that read 'accept' and 'ignore' seemed to be staring at Jenny.

"Not now," she said to herself and clicked on the 'ignore' button. Then she logged off *The Network*, shut down her computer and started to collect her things for school tomorrow.

CHAPTER TWO A new classmate

It was a quarter past eight when Jenny arrived at St Thomas More Roman Catholic School. She noticed the first signs of autumn on this September day. Some of the leaves were already turning yellow, and the morning was almost chilly, although it was to be quite warm again later.

Jenny felt a bit strange to be back after a long summer holiday. She was now in year eleven, which meant that this year she would be doing her GCSEs. She was not exactly bad at school, but a lot of her school reports ended with the comment: "Could do better". Still, no reason for her mother to be so worried about her, she thought.

Now she was waiting for Vicky, who had just sent her a text message saying that she would be five minutes late. Some of her friends and classmates had already arrived and were chatting in the schoolyard.

"Hi Jenny! How are you? Good to see you again!"

Jenny turned around. She hadn't noticed that two girls had approached her from behind. One of them was Emily Sheen, who had made the funny comment about her on *The Network*, and the other one was Haylie Walker.

"Hi Hale, hi Em!" Jenny muttered while they were giving each other kisses on their cheeks. She usually felt a little bit uncomfortable in the presence of the two girls, who always seemed to stick together like glue. Just between Jenny and Vicky, the two of them had the nickname "H&M". But still, they were all friends, at least on *The Network*. In reality, Jenny never really knew what to think of them, especially Haylie. She was nice enough to Jenny when they met, but there was always something about her that Jenny did not trust. Perhaps it was because Jenny once heard from a friend of a friend that Haylie had been talking about her behind her back.

"You're looking great!" Haylie grinned. "So, how was your holiday? Where did you go?"

Jenny tried to avoid eye-contact with Emily. "Well, I didn't do much. Didn't go anywhere. Basically, I just relaxed. You know, slept late, met some friends. Went to a party. Well, actually I went to Southend with my mum for a weekend, but I'm not sure if you can call that a holiday."

"Yeah, that's what you wrote on *The Network*. I just thought there might have been something you didn't want to let everybody know."

Jenny thought about Haylie's comment for a moment, but she did not quite understand what she meant.

"Anyway, guess where we went?" Haylie went on proudly. "You won't believe this! Dad took us all on a last-minute trip to Florida! We went to this fantastic holiday resort in Miami Beach for two weeks!"

Another reason why Jenny did not really like Haylie was that her parents seemed to be quite wealthy. And perhaps it was also because Haylie actually had more than one parent.

"Wait, you've got to see this!" Haylie said. She took out her smartphone and touched the screen to unlock it. Her fingers flew over the display quickly as she flicked through her collection of photos.

"Now, this is our hotel. Look at this pool! Right … this is the view from our balcony. And this is the beach! It was fantastic! But it was really hot …!"

Looking at all the photos that could have been taken from a holiday brochure, Jenny began to feel frustrated.

"Speaking of hot, I've got to show you this!"

Haylie held her smartphone close to Jenny's face. The display was small, but Jenny was able to recognize Haylie in a bikini on the beach, smiling from ear to ear. Next to her was a well-built, good-looking boy of about sixteen or seventeen who had his arm around Haylie's shoulder. His broad grin showed a long line of perfect white teeth.

"Now, this is Danny! He's actually from New York. I tell you, he's so cute, and he's such a good laugh! Look at this one … and this is where we used to meet in the evenings. And this is Danny in his car – did you know they're allowed to drive at sixteen in the US? – and here we are …"

Jenny had stopped listening. Her mind was wandering off. Why did everybody else always seem so much luckier than her?

"… he told me that he wants to study in London when he's finished high school. Well, his father has a law firm in New York, so I guess he will be paying for his stay in the UK. Danny and me are keeping in touch through *The Network*. I'll post all the pictures first thing this afternoon. Oh, sorry Jenny, there's Nick, I've gotta say hi to him. Laters!"

"Yeah, see you later," Jenny called after the two girls as they walked away to talk to another boy who had just arrived. She was glad that they all had to wear uniforms at school so Haylie could not show off all the fashionable clothes she had. Jenny was still lost in thought when she suddenly heard someone talking to her.

"Hi Jenny! How's things with you?"

"Oh, hi Vicky! Well, could be better, to be honest."

"Why? What's happened?" Vicky asked, looking a bit worried. "Anything to do with H&M?"

"Dunno. Yes and no. Maybe."

"Tell me, what's up?"

"Oh well, Haylie's just showed me pictures of her fantastic summer holiday, and she also seems to have chatted up a great guy. I mean, good for her, but in the meantime I was staying in fantastic Wood Green, having arguments with my mother! That's not exactly fair, is it?"

"I know what you mean," Vicky said, trying to sound more understanding than usual. "But you know what she's like."

"Anyway, perhaps Mum's right," Jenny continued. "It's all Dad's fault. If he hadn't run off with another woman, we would probably be a happy family that could live a normal life like everybody else. Or he would take us on a special holiday, like Haylie's dad. But he's never even tried to contact me! What kind of a dad is that?"

Vicky did not quite know what to say. She looked at Jenny, and then she said, "Well, that's difficult for me to answer. But sometimes you just don't know why things are the way they are. Have you actually never tried to contact *him*?"

"Me?" Jenny almost shouted. "Why should I try to contact him? It was him who ran away, wasn't it? I think if anybody has to make a move, it's him!"

"Yeah … I suppose you're right," Vicky said, thinking of something to say to change the subject. "Anyway, did you manage to revise French?"

"Well, just a bit," Jenny said as she was calming down again. "But it got a bit late because I wanted to sort out the party pictures on *The Network* first. Oh, by the way, that reminds me: who was this Kevin guy who came along to the cinema last Saturday? I mean, where do you know him from?"

"Oh, I got to know him through *The Network*. He's friends with Alan, so I thought it might be a good idea to accept him as a friend."

"Yeah, that does sound like a good idea," Jenny said slowly.

"Then we started chatting," Vicky went on. "He lives quite close to me, so we met up the next day."

"You went out with someone you had just met on *The Network*?" Jenny asked as if she couldn't believe what she had just heard.

"Why not? Well, we didn't really go out, I mean, it wasn't a date or anything. We only went to *Stardust's* in High Road for a quick drink in the afternoon."

"But you didn't really know him," Jenny said. "And he doesn't look like your type of guy," she added.

"You don't always have to fancy someone to be nice and friendly to them, do you?" Vicky replied. "I think you can actually tell from the way people chat what kind of person they are. And Kevin just seemed nice enough to me. He's at Woodside High School. Don't know why because he's actually quite clever. Well, a bit of a computer nerd, to be honest, but as I said, he's quite nice. I had problems with my laptop the other day, and he offered to help me. I went to his place, and he managed to fix it in only half an hour! That's why I asked him if he wanted to come and see *Twilight* with us. But why are you asking me about him?"

Jenny thought for a moment of what to say, but then she just muttered, "Nothing special. I was just interested."

Their conversation was interrupted by the sudden ringing of the school bell. It was ten to nine now, and they all had to go to their form rooms for registration. Students were pushing and shoving through the corridors, and everything got much noisier. Jenny had not missed this at all in the past six weeks.

Mr Appleyard, their form teacher, welcomed all the students and started to tick off their names. Jenny looked around to see all the familiar faces. Some of them had a suntan or a new haircut. A few students looked somehow older, but most of them hadn't changed at all. Suddenly she noticed that there was a boy standing near the wall, half behind Mr Appleyard. He was tall and slim with ginger hair. He was standing still, and his eyes and mouth did not move.

"Right," Mr Appleyard said when he was finished with his list of names. "Now let me just introduce Mark Kelly, who moved here from Cork in Ireland this summer and who will be joining us from now on. I hope you will show him that St Thomas More students are well-known for their good manners and friendly behaviour."

Some of the students sneered and giggled. Mr Appleyard was now looking a bit upset. "I am quite sure you've all understood me," he said and turned to the new boy. "Now, Mark, perhaps you'd like to sit at that table over there."

Without a word, Mark walked to a table in the back of the classroom where nobody else was sitting. He sat down, his eyes and mouth still not moving.

"Right," Mr Appleyard said, "let's start."

It was ten past eleven. Jenny had been waiting for this moment the whole morning in class. Break had just started, and they were out in the schoolyard again.

"At last," Jenny groaned. "I just can't get used to being back at school. Appleyard is getting more and more annoying. He's got no sense of humour. And why does he have to go on about our GCSEs on our first day back at school?"

"Well, I guess he wants to make us work harder this year," Vicky replied. "After all, it's his job."

They were now walking across the schoolyard. Most of their classmates were standing together in small groups, chatting. Some younger students were running around, screaming and chasing each other. Vicky looked around and noticed Mark leaning against the wall of the schoolyard, staring into the distance. He almost looked as if he was asleep with eyes wide open.

"What do you think of the new guy, Mark?" Vicky asked Jenny.

"The Paddy? Dunno. He hasn't even said anything yet," Jenny replied absent-mindedly.

"Oh, come on, Jenny! It's rude to call him 'Paddy'!" Vicky said. "I guess it's not easy for him, being in a new place without friends. Just imagine you had to move to Cork and go to a new school there. What would you do? I'm sure he feels lonely here."

"Lonely?" Jenny said, fully focused again. "I'm sure he's moved here with his five brothers or sisters. They all have big families in Ireland. And I guess most of them have a mum *and* a dad."

Vicky realized she had again pushed a button with Jenny.

"It's easy for Irish people to make new friends," Jenny continued. "I bet he's already been to the *Shannon Arms* Irish pub. That's where all the Irish hang out. And anyway, he can always keep in touch with his old mates through *The Network.*"

Vicky was staring at Jenny. "Can you hear yourself?" she finally said. "The *Shannon Arms* is a shabby place where all the yobs hang out! You know that! What's wrong with you, Jenny? Why are you in such a bad mood?"

Jenny did not know what to say, and she was beginning to feel a bit ashamed of what she had just said.

"Right," Vicky said. "Let's just go and talk to him!"

She grabbed Jenny by the hand and walked over to where Mark was standing. When he noticed the two girls coming towards him, he slowly lifted his head and looked at them apprehensively.

"Hi!" Vicky said. "So, how do you like this place?"

Mark did not answer straight away but first looked at Jenny, and then at Vicky.

"'Ts alright," he finally muttered. It was the first words they both heard from him, but Jenny immediately noticed a strong Irish accent.

"It's actually not so bad, you'll see," Vicky tried to cheer Mark up, but it did not really seem to work.

"I'm Vicky, by the way, and this is Jenny."

Jenny tried to give a friendly smile. "Hi!"

"Hi Jenny. How's the form?" Mark said.

"The form?" Jenny asked back, looking puzzled. "What do you mean, our class?"

"No," said Mark, and for the first time something like a faint smile appeared on his face. "That's how we say 'how are you' where I come from. I'm sorry, I've really gotta get used to speaking differently."

"Well, your English sounds OK to me," Vicky smiled. "So, when did you come over here?"

"About two weeks ago," Mark answered. The ice was broken now. "We now live, like, on Myddleton Road. But my uncle lives in Wembley, so I've spent quite a bit of time in that part of London. Haven't really seen much of Wood Green so far."

"You haven't missed much," Jenny interrupted, ignoring Vicky's irritated look. "So what made you come here? I mean, to Wood Green, of all places? I thought Cork was said to be really nice."

Mark's smile faded away as quickly as it had appeared. He was now wearing the same expression on his face as when he was introduced to his new class.

"It's for job reasons," he finally muttered, when suddenly the school bell started ringing again.

"Well, anyway, if you need any help with anything, just let us know," Vicky said.

"Thanks," Mark said. "That would be awesome."

His face brightened up again, and, like all the others, the three of them went back to their classroom.

School was over at last. Jenny was back home in her room. She had switched on her computer and was now waiting for it to boot up. She had quite a bit of homework to do: a couple of Maths exercises, a French text to prepare, and two pages of History to read. After about five or six minutes, her computer was ready for use.

First, Jenny opened her e-mail program. She clicked on the 'receive' button and, about thirty seconds later, her inbox was filled with fourteen new e-mails: three newsletters from some online fashion shops, a message from Alex Lawson that had two bad film reviews of *Twilight* attached to it, and ten more spam e-mails.

"Why are you always trying to sell me this bloody Viagra?" Jenny said angrily as she was deleting all the spam e-mails. "I'm a girl, you stupid idiots!"

She closed the e-mail program and logged on to *The Network*. There were a few more comments on Vicky's party pictures, but none of them were really interesting or annoying. Jenny felt relieved.

She scrolled down to her *Network* message inbox. A new message had been sent by Haylie: "Hi everyone! If you want to see what a real holiday looks like, click HERE!"

"I don't want to see your stupid photos," Jenny thought and clicked on the link that directed her to Haylie Walker's *Network* profile, straight to the folder that contained all her Florida pictures. In high definition, of course. Jenny looked at every single one of them. Haylie's holiday must have been more than fantastic: sunshine, a wide open beach, a posh hotel room and a guy called Danny who looked even better than on Haylie's smartphone display.

Jenny went back to Haylie's comment section and opened a new comment line. "Lucky you!" she typed in but then stopped and thought about it for a few minutes. She finally deleted the message and started again. "Big deal, with rich parents like yours!" was her second comment, but again she deleted it before she pressed the 'Enter' key. Her mind was blank.

While she was thinking about what to write, she suddenly noticed that the small icon of her own *Network* profile at the bottom of the screen was flashing. She clicked on it, and a new window suddenly popped up.

"Kevin wants to invite you to a chat".

"Him again," Jenny thought. "All right then, let's be nice today."

She clicked on the 'accept' button. The window changed its shape. Now there was a picture of Kevin in the top left-hand corner, while her own one was on the right. Below the two pictures was a field where the dialogue between the two was about to appear.

Kevin: "hi, how are you?"

Jenny: "Fine, thanks. And you?"

Kevin: "not too bad thanks."

"This is going to be an exciting conversation", Jenny thought to herself while she was waiting for the next line to appear on her screen. She didn't really like chatting because you never knew when someone was going to post a line, so sometimes messages could overlap. A way to avoid this was to send longer messages in small chunks, which was exactly what Kevin was doing now.

Kevin: "i really enjoyed the cinema on saturday"

Kevin: "with you lot. i quite liked the film."

Kevin: "i just thought it was a pity we didnt"

Kevin: "really have time to chat so"

Kevin: "i thought it might be best"

Kevin: "if i contact u on the network."

Kevin: "i hope u dont mind."

Jenny was waiting for more text to arrive, but Kevin seemed to be expecting a reply now, so she just typed in: "No, not at all."

Kevin: "btw the second twilight film is on next"

Kevin: "week so i was wondering if youd"

Kevin: "like to go."

Now Jenny was not quite sure what to write. Was this going to be a date? Or was he just being nice, as Vicky had said? Jenny then had an idea.

Jenny: "So how do you know Alan Shearer?"

Kevin: "hes just a friend of my brothers"

Jenny: "Are they good friends?"

Kevin: "they play on the same football team"

Jenny: "Do you sometimes hang out with him too?"

Kevin: "i have done. why r u asking?"

Jenny: "Do you think he would like to come along to the cinema?"

There was no reply. Kevin seemed to be thinking. Finally, after what seemed like several minutes, a new line appeared.

Kevin: "i dont think thats such a good idea."

Kevin: "i think i heard he didnt like the first film."

Jenny: "Why don't you just ask him?"

Kevin: "i suppose i could do that."

Kevin: "so do you want to go?"

Jenny: "Let me think about it."

Again, there was no immediate reply from Kevin. Jenny was getting a bit tired with this chat. She somehow felt that Kevin was probably not as useful as she had thought to get in touch with Alan, so she decided to end the conversation.

Jenny: "Sorry Kevin, I've got to go now. Talk to you later."

She clicked on the 'end' button and the chat window disappeared. Jenny took a deep breath. Then she scrolled up again, opened a new comment line and started to write.

"School was awful. Appleyard's a nightmare. And we got sooo much homework on our first day!"

When she typed in the last sentence, Jenny realized that she still had not started her homework. It was a quarter past six now. She had better get started before her mother was home from work.

Suddenly, a new window popped up.

"Kevin wants to invite you to a chat".

"What does he want now?" Jenny thought. "Hmm. Perhaps he's changed his mind – or maybe Alan will come along to the cinema after all?"

She clicked on the 'accept' button again and the chat window opened.

Kevin: "hi, its me again."

Jenny: "Yes, I can see that."

Kevin: "im sorry to bother u again. perhaps"

Kevin: "the cinema isnt such a good idea after all."

Kevin: "if u want i thought we might"

Kevin: "meet up for a drink some time?"

Kevin: "theres a nice cafe in High Road."

Jenny was beginning to feel a bit annoyed. What had started as a clever way of approaching Alan Shearer now seemed to be becoming a date with a boy she did not fancy at all. Why on earth did Vicky meet up with this guy? And why did Vicky not mention to her how forward Kevin could be? Was this really the same Kevin she had met at the cinema? Jenny had no answer to all these questions, but she was determined to stop this chat now.

Jenny: "Really gotta go. Bye."

She clicked on the 'end' button and, once again, the window disappeared. Jenny sat there and stared at the screen. Somehow this was not her day, she thought. Then she noticed that Haylie's *Network* profile was still open. She clicked on it and found herself back at Haylie's comment section. People had started to comment on Haylie's holiday pictures.

"Lucky you!" someone had posted. Jenny sighed. She noticed that Haylie's new friend Danny was now at the top of her list.

She closed Haylie's *Network* profile and looked at her own comment line she had started to write: "... we got sooo much homework on our first day!" Again, it reminded her that she had quite a bit of homework to do. Her mother could be back any minute.

Jenny stopped thinking about any possible changes to her comment. She just pressed 'Enter'. A few seconds later, the comment appeared as a new entry on her profile, and a window popped up.

"Kevin wants to invite you to a chat".

"For God's sake! This is definitely too much now!" Jenny shouted.

Without further thought she clicked on 'ignore', and the window disappeared again.

Jenny looked at her *Network* profile. She could still see Kevin's picture on the left-hand side, among her long list of friends. She slowly moved the mouse over the picture. A drop-down menu opened. There were all kinds of labels you could attach to your friends, such as 'close friend', 'family' and so on. At the bottom of the menu, it said 'unfriend'. Jenny clicked on it.

"Do you want to unfriend Kevin?" a new pop-up message said.

"Definitely!" Jenny replied as she clicked on 'yes'. "This wasn't going anywhere."

She looked at her list that now had 127 friends. It was the first time that it had got smaller. Suddenly she heard some noise from downstairs.

"Hi Darling!" Jenny's mum shouted. "I'm back!"

"Hi Mum!" Jenny shouted back, but not very loudly.

She quickly closed all the open windows on her computer screen and unpacked her textbooks. She had just finished spreading her French books on her desk when there was a knock on the door.

"Come in!" Jenny shouted.

"Hello Dear," her mum said when she came into the room. "How was school today?"

"It was OK," Jenny said. There was a moment of silence.

"I'm really sorry about last night," her mother finally began as she sat down on Jenny's bed, which was right next to her desk. "You know, things are really stressful at work at the moment."

"I know, Mum," Jenny said, trying to show some understanding. She had heard it all before, but still she was pleased that her mother had come to apologize.

www.thenetwork.com
Jenny Anderson
Connect with People
Find Friends
The Network
Welcome
News
Events
Find Friends
The Network
The Network
Do you want to unfriend Kevin?
No
Yes
Kevin
Family
Unfriend
Exit
Add as Friend
Add as Friend

"It's no fun being a single mother, and I really want to make sure that this won't happen to you. Well, you can never be sure with men, of course, so if it does happen, you should at least have a good job that keeps you going."

"Yeah, I suppose you're right," Jenny said quietly. She looked at her mother. "Mum?"

"Yes, Dear?"

"Will you tell me more about Dad sometime? I mean, some more details, what exactly happened and why, and so on."

"I will," she said and gave her a kiss. "Sometime. But let me just go and make dinner now."

Mrs Anderson got up and walked out of Jenny's room. Jenny turned to her desk. Time for French now. It had to be done.

About twenty minutes later, Jenny had more or less prepared the French text and was now having a go at the Maths exercises. They seemed impossible to solve, no matter how hard she tried. She was getting more and more frustrated.

She went back to her computer, opened her *Network* profile and typed in a message: "Does anybody know how to do these b****y Maths exercises? Solutions are most welcome!"

She pressed 'Enter' and stared at the screen. *The Network* had been helpful before because sometimes one of Jenny's classmates was nice enough to share their homework with everyone online. But this time, instead of giving her any ideas about Maths, a message popped up saying, "Mike wants to be your friend".

"Mike?" Jenny thought. "Who's this then?"

She clicked on the link, and her computer started working hard to direct her to Mike's *Network* profile. When it had finally finished, Jenny could not believe her eyes.

"Wow!" she said out loud. There was a picture of an incredibly good-looking boy of about seventeen or eighteen years with short, dark hair. His large, dark eyes were squinting, and he had a confident smile on his face.

Jenny began to click on every icon or link on his *Network* profile. There was not too much information. He was interested in some of the same music as Jenny and seemed to do a lot of sport. His full name was Mike Armstrong, he was in fact eighteen years old and was living on White Hart Lane in Tottenham. There were only five people on his list of friends, all of them good-looking and about the same age. He clearly seemed to choose his friends very carefully, Jenny thought.

The most interesting piece of information was that he had already finished school and was now trying to become a professional photographer. There were several picture folders with different names, like 'landscapes', 'cars' or 'animals'. Jenny clicked on the folder that was labelled 'female models'. It contained about ten pictures of some beautiful young girls that were about her age, or perhaps a little bit older. All the photos looked very professional.

"Do we want to be friends? Yes, we do," Jenny smiled as she clicked the OK button. Soon, a new pop-up message announced: "You are now friends with Mike!" Jenny was pleased to see that her list of friends was back to 128. Then she returned to Mike's *Network* profile.

"I'd love to see Haylie's face when she discovers Mike on my list of friends," Jenny thought.

Lost in thought, she was slowly clicking around Mike's profile. She decided to save his picture on her computer. "I could send this straight on to Vicky by e-mail," she thought. Suddenly, the door to her room opened.

"Jenny! Can't you hear me? I've already called you three times!"

Like waking up from a dream, Jenny turned around quickly and looked at her mother.

"Dinner's ready. And do switch that computer off! It's *The Network* again, isn't it? Oh, Jennifer, what am I going to do with you?"

CHAPTER FOUR Working out

It was Jenny's second day back at school after the summer holidays. She still felt a bit uncomfortable when she entered the schoolyard. Perhaps it was because she knew that this was going to be a hard year for her, and the fact that she had not managed to do yesterday's Maths homework certainly added to her bad feeling. Vicky was already waiting for her.

"Hi Jenny! How are you?" Vicky smiled.

"I'm fine, thanks. How about yourself?" Jenny replied.

"I'm OK, thanks. Did anyone send any ideas on how to do Maths? I saw your cry for help on *The Network*. Sorry, but I couldn't answer the questions myself."

"No," Jenny said. "No ideas this time. I'm beginning to wonder if our teachers are doing this on purpose. I mean, show us how little we know so we work harder for our GCSEs. But that's no help at all."

Vicky just nodded.

"Well, I had hardly any time to do the homework anyway because I kept being bothered by this Kevin guy," Jenny continued. "You know, I stupidly accepted him as a friend on *The Network*, and he just tried to chat me up immediately! Can you believe it?"

"You don't say," Vicky said, staring at Jenny.

"It's true! He kept trying to ask me out on a date, so I finally unfriended him. I really don't understand why he was so different. I mean, at the cinema he didn't say a word to me, but when we were chatting online he wasn't shy at all."

"I think I know what you mean," Vicky said. "I thought more or less the same thing. When we were chatting on *The Network,* he seemed quite confident, with a good sense of humour, but when we actually met up, he was much more nervous and quiet. Still, I think he's a nice guy."

"Makes you wonder why he's friends with Alan," Jenny said almost to herself. "He's certainly not much use for getting in contact with Alan."

Vicky gave Jenny a surprised look. Jenny felt like she had just been caught revealing a secret.

"Anyway," Jenny went on quickly, "I'm not really interested in Alan. I don't need to be. Hey, listen, you won't believe this: I got contacted by a fantastic guy called Mike Armstrong! He's really good-looking! He's eighteen, from Tottenham, and a professional photographer. You should see some of his pictures, they're awesome! Just have a look at my *Network* site if you want to see him."

"Sounds too good to be true," Vicky said, sounding a lot less excited than Jenny. "But why should he contact you? Have you checked his list of friends?"

"Of course I have," Jenny replied, "but I don't know any of them. At least not yet. Perhaps he's just looking for new models he can take pictures of?"

Vicky was beginning to feel annoyed by Jenny's unexpected rise in self-confidence. They were friends, best friends, but this did not mean that there was no hidden rivalry between the two. Jenny was quite a good-looking girl, and usually the boys found her more attractive than Vicky. Still, Jenny somehow always managed to stay without a boyfriend. Perhaps, Vicky thought, this was because of Jenny's way of behaving sometimes, which seemed to be too close to arrogance.

"Well, I'd certainly be a bit careful," Vicky finally said.

"Careful?" Jenny snarled. "You, of all people, are telling me to be careful? You, who went out with this stupid nerd Kevin straight away, are telling me to be careful? The guy can't even write properly!"

"All right, but at least I knew that he was friends with Alan," Vicky tried to calm her down.

"Friends with Alan," Jenny sneered. "They're not really friends! They hardly know each other!"

The argument was suddenly interrupted by Mark, who had slowly walked up to them. He was now standing right next to the two girls.

"Hi. How's the … er, how are you?" Mark said.

"Fine, thanks," both Jenny and Vicky replied together. "Apart from the fact that we didn't manage to do the Maths exercises," Jenny added.

"Oh, yeah, that was, like, a bit tricky. I had almost forgotten how to do it, but I still have my old exercise books, so I just looked everything up. Do you want to copy the answers?"

Jenny and Vicky looked at each other.

"You managed to do it?" Jenny finally said.

"To be sure! We did the stuff in Ireland last year, and we had a pretty good teacher, so it was a piece of cake. Wait, I'll show you."

About ten minutes later, Mark had explained the basics of the Maths exercises clearly and simply, and the two girls had copied everything into their own exercise books.

"Fantastic!" Vicky said. "I mean, of course it would've been better to have done it all ourselves, but I'm sure this will earn us some brownie points in Maths. And that's what we need at the start of the year, isn't it?"

"Yeah, definitely," Jenny agreed. "Thanks, Mark."

"No worries," said Mark. "Actually, perhaps you can do me a favour too. I used to go to, like, a swimming club in Cork, and I'd like to continue my training here. So, do you know a good pool in this area?"

"A good swimming pool?" Vicky repeated, looking at Jenny. "Arnos Pool is quite good, isn't it? That's near your place, Jenny. Hey, I tell you what: why don't we all go there this afternoon? Then we can show Mark where everything is. I haven't been there for ages."

"That would be awesome," Mark said, smiling shyly. "I mean, are you sure it won't bother you too much?"

"Not at all," Vicky said. "Let's meet at Jenny's place at four."

Jenny did not quite know what to say. She thought that Vicky's openness was sometimes a bit too much, but it was too late to backtrack now.

"So, where do you live?" Mark asked carefully.

"Oh, I live at 26 Herbert Road," Jenny said. "That's right next to Bowes Park train station. You can cross the railway at Ireland Place. You should know that place, shouldn't you? Anyway, it's next to Myddleton Road, so it must be quite near where you live."

"I know," Mark said. "I've been there. Ireland Place sounded nice to me, so I had a look at it when I was exploring the area. So, I'll be at your place at four."

"I'll send you a text message before," Jenny added almost automatically.

"Why?" Mark asked, looking a bit surprised. "When I say I'll be there, I'll be there. See you at four then."

He walked off. Jenny turned to Vicky.

"Well, is this going to be a date for you?"

"Come on, Jenny!" Vicky sighed. "This is not a date! You've got to learn to be nicer to people. And anyway, didn't you mention the other day that you need to slim down and get fit?"

It was ten to four. Jenny was in her room. She had packed all her swimming things and was now waiting for Vicky and Mark to arrive. She was still feeling a bit uncomfortable about going to the pool with Mark, but at least Vicky was with her.

"Hopefully, Vicky will be here before Mark," Jenny thought when she suddenly heard a beep coming from her mobile phone. Vicky had sent her a text message.

"Hi Jenny, sorry can't make it. Forgot that I have to babysit. Enjoy the pool! CU Later."

"Oh no!" Jenny shouted out. She felt a sudden flash of heat inside her. What to do now? Send Mark a text and call it off? Not possible, as she did not have his mobile number. Tell him she was feeling sick? Probably not very convincing. Suddenly, the door bell rang.

When she opened the door, Mark was sitting on quite a cool mountain bike, smiling at her.

"Hi! Ready to go?" he said.

"Er, yes, I'll just get my things," Jenny replied. "Oh, by the way, Vicky's just texted me to say she can't make it. I can show you the message."

Mark laughed. "Don't. I'll believe you. Are we going by bike?"

"Well, I don't think so," Jenny said. "I've got a bike, but I haven't used it for a while. It's got a puncture. We can walk. It's not very far. Do you want to put your bike in the hallway? It looks pretty expensive."

"That would be great," he said and pushed his bike inside.

A few minutes later, Mark and Jenny were walking along Brownlow Road. Arnos Pool was about twenty minutes away. There was an awkward silence, and Jenny had to think hard of something to say.

"Your school in Cork must have been quite good if you've already done the Maths stuff," she finally said. "Why did you choose to come to our school?"

"Well, it was the only Roman Catholic school in the area, and my mum thought this was, like, kind of important."

"Oh," Jenny replied, thinking about whether it would be wise to go on asking about it. She decided to change the subject.

"Perhaps it would've been good to have your mobile number, just in case. I realised I couldn't contact you."

"Oh, sure," Mark said. "No problem. But I hardly use it. Just in an emergency. I've only got a pay-as-you-go phone."

"Really?" Jenny asked, surprised. "I suppose you prefer keeping in touch through *The Network* then. I can add you as a friend, if you want."

"*The Network*?" Mark asked, just as surprised. "I've heard of that, but I've never used it."

Jenny was beginning to think that Mark was perhaps a bit odd after all. Or was it just that the Irish were a bit old-fashioned?

"But you do have the internet in Ireland, don't you?" she grinned, and her voice revealed that she was being rather sarcastic.

Mark did not seem to find this too funny. He just did not reply, and their conversation was back to the first stage of awkward silence. Again, Jenny was thinking of something to say when they came past a shabby-looking pub.

"Er, this is the *Shannon Arms*, by the way. It's quite a well-known Irish pub in this area," she finally managed to come up with.

"Is it any good?" Mark asked, realising that he had to help Jenny continue the conversation.

"No, actually, not at all. Lots of yobs. I'm sure the pubs in Ireland are better. Must be, because it can't be much worse than this one. Anyway, look, we're almost there."

They finally arrived at Arnos Pool. Jenny was glad that she was able to be on her own again for a while. She got changed, had a shower and went into the hall where the pool was. She was now feeling more than uncomfortable. There were a few people in the pool swimming laps. Arms crossed in front of her, Jenny quickly walked towards the pool and jumped into it. She began to swim. After what felt like five minutes she had managed to do one length and back. She stopped at the shallow end, panting. She could not believe how unfit she was. Next to her, in the fast lane, someone was sliding through the water like a fish. It turned out to be Mark, who stopped when he saw Jenny standing in the water at the end of the pool.

"Hey, this is a great pool!" he said and smiled from ear to ear as he lifted his goggles. "How are you doing? Are you more into breaststroke or front crawl?"

Jenny noticed two things immediately. Firstly, Mark seemed to be a completely different person; he was a lot happier and more relaxed than on their way to the pool.

And secondly, he looked quite athletic now that his body was not covered by the wide shirts he was usually wearing.

"Oh, I can only do breaststroke, or at least I try to. I've never really understood how to do front crawl. It's quite tiring, isn't it?"

"Not really, if you do it properly. You just have to make sure that you..."

Mark began to tell Jenny in detail all the things she had to think about when doing front crawl. He gave her his goggles to have a look from underwater how he was using his arms and turning his head to breathe. Jenny was listening and watching, but she had the feeling that she was not really taking in the information. Still, she did not feel bored at all.

"Right," Mark finally said. "Now try yourself."

Jenny tried to remember what Mark had told her, but her version of front crawl looked as useless as ever.

"No! Lift your arms more," he laughed. "OK, let's do some practice at the shallow end."

Mark was standing in the water, holding his arms out. He asked Jenny to lie flat on the water, face down, doing the arm movements while he was holding her from below like a swimming instructor. Jenny did as she was told, but now she could not even lift her arms. She felt like a big, wet sack of rice. For some reason, her mind was not focused on swimming any more.

"All right," Mark finally said. "Don't worry, it takes a lot of time and practice. Shall we go?"

Back home Jenny felt strange. She could not quite figure out what it was. She tried to phone Vicky but could not reach her. She decided to write her a text message but

stopped after three words. Jenny's mind was blank, even though her brain was fully active. Soon her mother came home and entered the room to say hello to her. Jenny did not say anything about Mark. Instead, she told her that she had been to the pool with Vicky to get fit and, to her surprise, her mother did not give her the usual talk about doing her homework. Jenny felt very tired, and when she was finally lying in bed, she realized that she had forgotten to check her *Network* profile the whole evening.

CHAPTER FIVE The date

"I'm really sorry about the whole thing, honestly," Vicky said to Jenny as they were entering the schoolyard. "I should check my diary more carefully before making plans. Anyway, the babysitting was really boring. I guess the pool was much more fun. How was it, then?"

"Oh, it was nice," Jenny replied.

Vicky was staring at her, waiting for more information that just did not come.

"What do you mean, nice?" she asked. "The weather? The pool? Or Mark?"

Jenny did not answer straight away. "Everything," she finally said. "I mean, yes, Mark is actually nicer than I'd thought. He tried to teach me how to do front crawl, but I was completely hopeless. He was really patient with me. Actually, he's a very good swimmer."

"So?" Vicky asked, giving Jenny a long, meaningful look.

"Nah," Jenny said when she realised what Vicky meant. "He's nice, that's all. Wasn't it you who said you don't have to fancy someone to be nice and friendly to them? And anyway, in a way he's also a bit weird. He doesn't even know *The Network*!"

"Hmm. Perhaps they don't have the internet in Ireland," Vicky said, and Jenny was not quite sure whether she was being serious.

"Anyway," Jenny said to change the subject, "speaking of *The Network*: did you check out Mike's profile? What do you think of him?"

"Well," Vicky said, looking more serious now, "he's definitely a handsome guy. But what I noticed is that anyone can see his profile. I mean, it's not restricted to his friends or anything. That's strange. And why should he want to add you as a friend? As I said: it all looks too good to be true to me. So if I were you, I'd be a bit careful."

"Oh, come on," Jenny smiled at Vicky. "It's not unusual to keep your profile open for everyone if you have nothing to hide. I mean, he probably wants a lot of people to see his pictures. You just sound like you're a bit jealous. Why don't you admit it? I know that great guys are difficult to find, but … oh, hi Hale, hi Em! How are you?"

Vicky turned around to see that Haylie Walker and Emily Sheen were approaching where she and Jenny were standing.

"Shut up, fat bitch!" Emily said angrily as both girls walked quickly past them, looking in a different direction.

Jenny was puzzled, even shocked. "What's wrong with her?" she asked as she turned to Vicky. "Maybe she spotted Mike on my *Network* profile? Well, if she is jealous too, that's a bit of an overreaction!"

Vicky was looking even more serious now. "That's the other thing I wanted to tell you. You should be a bit more careful with the comments you post on your profile. The ones I read yesterday were not very nice."

"What?!" Jenny did not understand. "What do you mean? What comments?"

"Well," Vicky explained, "you basically made fun of some of the people who were at the party. And I remember that you insulted Emily in particular."

"I didn't!" Jenny shouted. She was getting nervous and worried now. "Why should I? When? I didn't! I was at the pool all afternoon, remember?"

Jenny was home at last. The whole day at school had been awful. She couldn't concentrate at all but had to think about what could have happened to her *Network* profile. While her computer was booting up, she was still hoping that what Vicky had told her was all just a joke. But Vicky was not the kind of person to play practical jokes.

When her computer was finally ready, she logged on to *The Network*. Jenny was shocked.

The first thing she saw was a pop-up message that simply read, "Three people have unfriended you." Below the message were the pictures of Emily, Haylie and Paul Bennington, another boy who was at the party two weeks ago.

She clicked the message away and noticed that her list of friends was now down to 125. It was not a joke then. The three of them were gone.

The next thing she noticed was that there were a lot of new messages in her comment section. Jenny took a deep breath and tried to stay calm. She decided to get to the bottom of this mystery, so she scrolled down to the last message she remembered writing herself. It was her message about the Maths exercises.

The next comment was also written by her, but it was dated 5 September, 4.14 pm. That was definitely when she was on her way to Arnos Pool with Mark. It was posted where the party pictures were. She started to read through the conversation that was right in front of her.

Jenny – 5 September at 4.14 pm: "I'm not chubby, you stupid bitch! Look at yourself! Have you never asked yourself why the boys don't like you?"

Emily – 5 September at 4.16 pm: "Oh, you sound like you know it's true … "

Jenny – 5 September at 4.17 pm: "The only thing that's true is that your're soooooo ugly! lol! Everyone at the party said that!"

Emily – 5 September at 4.18 pm: "Really? Are you sure they weren't talking about you instead?"

Jenny – 5 September at 4.18 pm: "I know what people said, but you don't! A lot of them are idiots and they were drunk because they can't take their drink! But still we all agreed: nobody likes you because you always tell other people's secrets. And because you're ugly!

Emily – 5 September at 4.21 pm: "That's it. I'm done with you. Have a nice life!"

Jenny – 5 September at 4.21 pm: "Go away then!"

Paul – 5 September at 5.37 pm: "Hey, I was at the party. What's going on, Jenny? It's not true what you're saying!"

Jenny – 5 September at 5.40 pm: "What do you know? You're just as stupid as all the others. I know you fancy me, but you can forget about that! I'm too pretty for you! You'll never be my boyfriend!"

Paul – 5 September at 5.42 pm: "Sorry, Jenny, I don't want to be, and I never did. You're mad!"

Jenny – 5 September at 5.43 pm: "Who cares?"

Jenny was breathing heavily. She could not believe what she saw with her own eyes. It was obvious what had happened. Someone must have logged on to her *Network* website and posted all those false messages in her name. But who? The only person who knew her password was

Vicky. Vicky could not have done that, or could she? Perhaps she had got really jealous and now wanted to hurt her. Impossible! Jenny just did not want to believe that her best friend would do something like that. Someone must have hacked into her account then. Perhaps it had something to do with her new friend, Mike? After all, Vicky had told her several times that she should be careful. Perhaps Mike did not exist, and he was just a virus or something like that? In any case, the best thing was to change her password immediately.

Suddenly Jenny realised that if someone was able to post messages on her profile in her name, he or she could of course do the same thing on her friends' *Network* profiles!

Jenny went through her list of friends. She had to check quickly whether anything had been posted there. Perhaps it was not yet too late to delete the messages? She first clicked on Mike's profile, but nothing had changed there. Everything was still the same. After she had checked her five most important friends, she felt a bit relieved. There were no more false messages from her. She clicked on the next contact when suddenly a window appeared.

"Mike wants to invite you to a chat".

Jenny's heart began to beat faster. What should she do now? So Mike was not a virus. Or was he? No, viruses cannot invite you to a chat. Well, maybe they can! Would it mess up her computer if she accepted? And what if this really was Mike? Anyway, she had to find out about all this now! Jenny had nothing to lose. She clicked on the 'accept' button.

Mike: "Hi, is that Jenny?"

Jenny: "Yes, it is. And you must be Mike?"

Mike: "Yes, I am. Sorry, is it OK to chat now?"

Jenny: "Yes, no problem. Good to hear from you."

Jenny was beginning to relax. Firstly, Mike was no virus, for sure. And secondly, he seemed to be nice.

Mike: "Perhaps you're wondering why I contacted you?"

Jenny: "Well, kind of. We don't seem to have any mutual friends".

Mike: "No, that's true. But I guess you know I'm a photographer?"

Jenny: "Yes, I've seen your pictures. I like them!"

Mike: "Thanks! Perhaps you've also seen the"

Mike: "models pics? I'm working for several"

Mike: "online fashion mags, and we're looking for"

Mike: "new faces. I found your profile here on *The*"

Mike: "*Network* and you look exactly like the type"

Mike: "of girl that Fashionline have asked for."

Jenny could not believe it. So what she had half-jokingly said to Vicky about Mike looking for new models was true! But just as she was getting excited, she remembered what Vicky had said. Jenny tried to stay calm.

Jenny: "You're not joking or anything?"

Mike: "No. I can imagine it sounds odd to you"

Mike: "but in my business we look for"

Mike: "new talent all the time."

Jenny: "Sounds too good to be true …"

Mike: "Actually, you can even earn a few quid"

Mike: "and if Fashionline likes the pics, there"

Mike: "may be follow-up jobs."

Jenny: "Hmm …"

Mike: "OK, if you're sceptical, why don't we"

Mike: "just meet up briefly and talk things over?"

Mike: "If you don't want to do it, it'd be a shame"

Mike: "but there are other girls queuing up."

Jenny suddenly felt nervous. Mike did not seem to be absolutely keen on her as a model, and she was now afraid of wasting the chance of her lifetime. It was now or never.

Jenny: "OK. When and where do you suggest?"

Mike: "I have a job at six, so what about five pm"

Mike: "today? We can meet somewhere in Wood"

Mike: "Green if you want."

Jenny: "OK. Let's say *Stardust's* in High Road."

Mike: "No problem, I know it. See you at five!"

Mike ended the conversation, and the chat window disappeared. Jenny was still feeling nervous. Five o'clock! That gave her about an hour to get ready. She switched off her computer. What on earth should she wear? Jenny looked into her wardrobe. All the clothes seemed old and shabby. She decided to wear the new summer dress she had bought last month. But how would she recognize him? Well, she had his picture, of course! And he had hers, so that could not be a problem. Jenny started to put on some make-up. Damn it! She had not asked for his mobile number! Switch on the computer again? No, it was probably too late. He must be on his way. Oh well, if he or she was late, so what? But was she being careful enough? Why not? Vicky had done exactly the same thing with someone who looked like more of a weirdo right from the start. And anyway, *Stardust's* was a public place, so no danger.

Jenny thought of the chance that was lying right in front of her. Perhaps this could become a profession after all? Then she would not have to worry about school and her GCSEs and everything any more. She took a final look in the mirror and left the house.

It was five o'clock sharp. Jenny had found a table at *Stardust's* coffee shop that gave her a good view of the entrance. She was holding on to her mobile phone nervously. Perhaps she should write Vicky a quick text message? Better not. Vicky was against all this anyway, and what if it all did not work out? Jenny decided to keep the whole date to herself. Was it a date, anyway?

More people were walking in and out, but none of them looked like Mike. It was ten past five now. Suddenly, a man in his forties walked up to her table and started to talk to Jenny.

"Excuse me," the man said, "you're Jenny Anderson, aren't you?"

Jenny was puzzled. "Er, yes," she said.

"Sorry to disturb you. My name is James Brunt. I'm a friend of Mike Armstrong's. Do you mind if I sit down?"

Without waiting for a reply, Mr Brunt sat down at Jenny's table and looked at her. He was wearing a suit and tie, and his hair was a bit grey at the sides. He looked like a typical businessman, but there was something about him that Jenny found strange.

"I'm glad I recognized you immediately," Mr Brunt continued. "Mike described you perfectly. Young, beautiful, with a face like Britney Spears. Just what Fashionline is looking for."

"So where is Mike?" Jenny interrupted him.

"Oh, sorry," Mr Brunt smiled. "Of course. Let me explain. Mike and I work for the same agency. I'm a photographer too. Well, let's say Mike's still learning, but I've been in the business for quite a while."

"So why is he not here now? He said he was going to meet me only an hour ago!" Jenny said impatiently.

"Well, you may not know our business," Mr Brunt went on. "It's quite hectic. Our schedules keep changing very quickly. Mike had another very important job come in just after he contacted you. It's something he had been waiting for, a really big job for him. So he asked me if I could take over this job with you from him. Well, he's done me favours before, so I thought it's my turn now."

Jenny was confused. What was going on here? It all sounded like a possible explanation, but this was not what she had expected. She did not know what to say or do. Should she do the whole thing with this man instead of Mike? After all, this was her great chance to become a model.

"Why don't we just meet up for a first photo shoot?" Mr Brunt asked, looking deep into Jenny's eyes. "Then you can get an idea of what it's all like. I would have time tomorrow, but if you're really flexible we could just as well start tonight."

"No!" Jenny shouted and got up from the table. "I'll do it with Mike or nobody! I'm leaving! I don't even know you!"

"Please, calm down," Mr Brunt said quietly. "No worries. There are still other girls for the job. But Mike won't have time any more, I can assure you. Perhaps you'll change your mind, and we can meet again some other time. Just call me."

Mr Brunt gave Jenny a piece of paper with a mobile phone number. Jenny took it almost automatically and, without saying anything more, turned around and quickly left the coffee shop.

BEVERAGES!
Coffee and Espresso
Caffè Misto
Caffè Americano
Caffè Latte
Cappuccino
Hot Chocolate
White Hot Chocolate
Steamed Apple Juice
Orange Mango Smoothie
Caffè Vanilla
Brewed Coffee
Decaf
Iced Coffee
Chai Latte
STAR DUST
COFFEE

Jenny was glad when she was back in her room. She had almost been running the whole way back from High Road. Now she was lying on her bed, and her eyes were filling with tears. Everyone and everything seemed to be against her!

After about ten minutes she had calmed down a little bit and was now thinking about what to do next. She had to contact Mike! Write him a message and ask him who this Mr Brunt was and why he could not meet her after all. Perhaps Mike had already written her a message to apologize for the whole thing? Jenny got up quickly and switched on her computer.

If Jenny had thought that this was a bad day and could not get any worse, she was wrong. When she opened her *Network* profile, she saw that another message had been posted. Posted in her name!

"Hey, wanna see more holiday pictures of me? Forget about Haylie, I'm the real beauty on the beach!" This time, the message was posted below a picture of an incredibly fat woman on a beach in a bikini that was far too tight for her. And the worst thing was: that woman had Jenny's face!

Jenny was almost feeling sick. She did not even take the trouble to read all the funny comments from other people that were below that false comment of hers. Someone must have manipulated the picture, using Jenny's face from some other picture. And that someone was still able to post messages and pictures in Jenny's name because she had been so excited to meet up with Mike that she had completely forgotten about changing her password!

It was almost impossible for Jenny to keep a clear head, but she somehow managed to think logically. First, she changed her password. She noted it down because she could not think of anything good, and she decided to change it again later. Then she started to delete the messages, comments and the picture, hoping that not too many people had already seen them.

When she had finished, she stared at the screen absent-mindedly. Anything else? Mike! Of course!

She looked through her list of friends, but instead of Mike's picture there was only a blank space. She clicked on it, and a new window opened.

"Sorry, this profile has been deleted."

Now Jenny was really feeling sick. What on earth did this mean? Thousands of different thoughts were going through her head at the same time now and were beginning to make some noise that she could not escape from. Then one particular noise became loud and clear.

"Jenny!!"

Mrs Anderson had entered the room.

"Are you deaf? Why don't you answer me? And for God's sake, stop playing with this *Network* thing and do your homework!"

CHAPTER SIX Private lessons

It was half past seven. Jenny was on her way to school. She had hardly slept. It was a bit earlier than usual because she had phoned Vicky last night and arranged to meet up with her to talk before school. Even though it was the beginning of September, summer seemed to have come back. It was going to be a hot day today.

When she entered the schoolyard, she looked around. There were only a handful of students there, but soon several buses would be coming and unloading students in large numbers. Jenny looked at the bus stop, which was about fifty metres away. She could see the backs of four or five people who were waiting for the next bus to arrive.

Suddenly she noticed that one of those people was actually looking in her direction. Jenny looked more closely, and what she saw made her heart almost stop. It was Mr Brunt!

Jenny turned around quickly. Her heart was now beating fast. She slowly moved out of view, pretending that she had not seen him. Had he seen her? Well, he must have! He had been looking directly at her! But what was he doing here in front of her school?

The first two buses arrived, and loads of students started to push and shove through the entrance. Jenny spotted two of her classmates, Anna and Maria. Seeing two familiar faces somehow felt good at this moment, but when Jenny said hi to them, they only grinned and walked past.

Now Jenny felt bad again. What was wrong with *these* two now? They were not exactly friends with H&M, even though they were, of course, all connected through *The*

Network. The only explanation was that they must have seen the false messages, too.

The crowd of students had moved on, and the buses had disappeared. Jenny slowly walked towards the entrance and turned around carefully from time to time to look at the bus stop. All the people had gone. She looked again. Nobody. Perhaps it had just been her imagination playing tricks on her, and the man had not been Mr Brunt after all. She felt a bit relieved.

Jenny walked back and saw Anna and Maria standing together with another classmate, Chris. They were all laughing. This was perhaps the time to explain a few things about what had happened to her profile. When she got nearer to them, she heard Anna say, "Oh, here she comes."

"Hey, you could at least say hi to me," Jenny started, trying not to look too annoyed.

"Oh, it's you, Jenny," Maria giggled. "I didn't recognize you. I thought you looked like this."

Maria held her smartphone close to Jenny's face, and she recognized the manipulated picture of her. Chris and Anna were laughing, but Jenny did not find this funny at all. What she had feared had become reality. The picture had started going around.

"Very funny!" Jenny said sarcastically. "Now, was it you who put this on my *Network* profile?"

"No, it was you, remember?" Maria said. "Like all the other stupid comments about Emily and the party."

"It wasn't me! Somebody else was pretending to be me!" Jenny shouted.

"That's what I would say if I had done something stupid like that," Maria replied. "I can see why Emily is angry with you."

Jenny did not know what to say any more. She was feeling really tired and did not have the strength to keep arguing. Just when she thought of something to say, she heard a beep in her pocket. She turned around and took her mobile out. Vicky had just sent her a text message saying that she would be five minutes late.

Jenny put her mobile away and turned around again, but Anna, Maria and Chris had moved away from her. Jenny was feeling frustrated and lonely now. Suddenly a familiar voice called her from behind.

"Hi Jenny! How are you?"

"Oh, hi Mark," Jenny said, and she was very happy to see him.

"So, how's Maths going? Do you need the homework for tomorrow?" Mark asked.

Jenny was suddenly reminded that she had not done much about her Maths homework, partly because she had been busy with *The Network*, partly because she felt more and more that she did not understand a thing that was going on in Maths.

"Er, yes, that would be very kind of you," she said. "But I'm not sure if this is actually a good solution. I mean, I can't keep copying your homework. I need to really understand this at some point. Remember, we're doing a class test next week."

"Hi you two!" a voice suddenly shouted. Vicky had just arrived. She was standing next to Jenny and Mark now, trying to follow the conversation that they were having.

Mark looked at Jenny. "I'll tell you what," he finally said. "Why don't we meet up today and I'll try my best to drum it into you, I mean, explain it to you."

"Really? Would you do that?" Jenny asked with wide open eyes.

"Well, why not?" he smiled. "I have an idea. Have you ever been to Alexandra Palace? It's near your place. I haven't managed to see it so far. We could perhaps have a look at it and then go for a picnic in Alexandra Park. It's such a nice day today, so why not do the work outside? I can get us some sandwiches to make our Maths lesson, like, more enjoyable."

"No way!" Jenny said, and Mark looked at her, puzzled. "*I'll* get the sandwiches. And some drinks. That's the least I can do if you are taking the trouble to explain boring Maths exercises to me."

Now Vicky was looking confused, and Mark was smiling again.

"Let's say four o'clock at my place again," Jenny said, and when Mark nodded, she continued, "Great! I'm looking forward to that. Now, I hate to say this, but Vicky and I were meeting up for some girls' talk. So if you don't mind ..."

"No worries," Mark said. "I'll see you at four at the latest." He turned around and walked off.

Vicky was staring at Jenny, waiting for an explanation.

"What?" Jenny asked impatiently. "Don't worry, it's only private lessons in Maths. Anyway, did you make up your mind about the whole *Network* story? Any idea what might have happened? Why did Mike delete his profile? And who was this James Brunt?"

At that moment, Jenny remembered seeing him this morning, but she decided to keep it to herself for now.

"Well, the big question is: does this Mike really exist?" Vicky asked Jenny, looking quite serious. "It looks very much like it was a false identity."

"Hmm ... don't know," Jenny said. She did not want to admit that she had actually been thinking the same. She was too afraid that her dream might just burst like a bubble.

"But who would do such a stupid thing?" Jenny asked. "I mean, what is the point?"

Vicky looked at Jenny, and Jenny could see that she seemed to have an idea but did not want to let it out.

"Jenny, you know what?" Vicky finally said. "I have a feeling that Kevin could be behind all this. I think we should meet up with him and try to find out about it."

"What? Kevin? Why him? And how? And anyway, what makes you say that?" Jenny asked.

"Oh, it's just a feeling," Vicky said absent-mindedly. "Anyway, even if it wasn't him, he might be able to help us. You know, he's a real computer nerd."

"All right. As long as he doesn't get excited about me," Jenny muttered, and this time Vicky was happy to see Jenny's self-confidence slowly coming back.

"Don't worry, I'll be there to hold your hand," Vicky smiled and was glad that Jenny found her comment quite amusing. "Let's go to his place tomorrow after school. I'll tell him this afternoon that there's something wrong with my laptop again. I won't tell him you're coming with me."

It all sounded like a good plan to Jenny. In any case, there was not much more she could do, and she was glad to have a real friend in Vicky.

Jenny was on her way back from school. She was still feeling bad because a lot of her classmates had ignored her the whole day. Now she was glad that she had something planned for this afternoon. Hopefully, it would take her mind off all her problems, and anyway, it was a good chance for her to catch up with Maths.

On her way, she stopped at a supermarket to get the picnic food. Four different types of sandwich and two bottles of cola. What else? What about some crisps?

Jenny reached down to one of the lower shelves and got two packets of cheese and onion crisps. When she got up again and turned around, a man was standing right in front of her. Jenny's heart almost stopped.

"Hello Jenny," Mr Brunt said. "What a surprise!"

Jenny was holding her shopping tight to her body. She wanted to speak but did not manage to say a single word.

"So," Mr Brunt continued, "have you made up your mind? It would be a shame to waste such a great chance, wouldn't it?"

Jenny's blood was slowly returning to her head and the rest of her body. Even though she was shaking with fear, she realized that this was also a chance to find out more about Mike.

"As I said before, I'd only do it with Mike. But I'm not sure any more if he actually exists. Or can you tell me why his *Network* profile was deleted?"

Mr Brunt started to laugh. "Young people are really funny! You know, even without a *Network* profile, people can still exist!"

He looked at Jenny in a way that gave her a weird feeling inside her stomach. "As I told you, he's got a big job going at the moment. I guess he just de-activated his account for a while so he could concentrate fully on his work. So, do you still want to think about the photo shoot? I hope you've still got my number, in case you change your mind."

"I said no! Leave me alone!" Jenny shouted and pushed past him. She just wanted to get out of the supermarket and run away. But she still had to get through the checkout. She tried to find the shortest queue. It seemed like the people in front of her were taking ages to pay for all their shopping.

Jenny tried to calm down. Nothing had happened. No worries! She looked around and saw that Mr Brunt was standing in another queue, looking at her. He smiled and made a sign to her that they should talk on the phone soon. Now Jenny felt sick again. She paid quickly, grabbed her shopping and hurried out of the supermarket.

Jenny was back in her room. She had taken a different, longer way home to make sure that Mr Brunt was not following her. Did he know where she lived? Probably not. How should he know that? But how did he know what school she was at? Hang on, it was not quite clear whether that man at the bus stop had been him. Or had he just followed her this morning?

While Jenny was trying to collect her thoughts, she realized that it was ten to four. Mark would be here soon. She had to get ready.

At four o'clock sharp, the door bell rang. For a brief moment, Jenny thought about Mr Brunt, but she opened the door and was relieved to see Mark on his mountain bike, smiling at her.

"Hi Jenny!" he said. "Are you ready? We're going by bike today."

"We can't. My bike's broken, I've told you", Jenny replied, but Mark only took out a puncture repair kit and held it up in the air.

A few minutes later, Mark was taking Jenny's bike apart while she was watching him with great interest. He seemed to know exactly what he was doing, and after a few more minutes, the puncture was gone and the bike back in full working order.

"Thank you so much," Jenny said slowly.

"You're welcome," Mark replied. "Let's go!"

Jenny felt a bit awkward on her bike. She had not used it for quite a while, but Mark was taking care that she was able to follow him. After about ten minutes, they arrived at Alexandra Palace.

"Wow," Mark said. "Isn't that a fantastic building? Look at the architecture. Typical Victorian style. Did you know that it was built in 1873 as a public leisure centre for the people? It was meant to be, like, North London's counterpart to the Crystal Palace in South London."

"No, I didn't," Jenny said. She almost felt ashamed that someone from as far away as Ireland was able to tell her something about her own neighbourhood.

"Later, it was used by the BBC as a television station," Mark continued. "See that radio tower? That's still in use."

"How do you know all these things?" Jenny asked with obvious surprise.

Mark smiled at her. "I read it on the internet."

"So you do have the internet?" Jenny asked, looking even more surprised.

"I never said I didn't. I just don't use *The Network*, Mark replied. "I prefer, like, the real world. Let's go down to the park now."

They found a nice place under a tree from where they had a great view of the London skyline. They lay down on the picnic blanket, and Mark started to explain the first few Maths exercises. Jenny was listening, but somehow she found it hard to concentrate. Everything felt so good: the weather, the place, and, for some reason, being with Mark. For the first time in what seemed like ages, Jenny was truly relaxed.

"Shall we take a break now?" Mark said, realizing that Jenny was not quite with it any longer.

"Yeah, why not. Have a sandwich." Jenny said.

"Thanks," Mark said and took a bite from the cheese sandwich. "So, tell me something about your family. Do you have any brothers or sisters?"

"No. I'm an only child," Jenny replied. "At least as far as I know. Don't know what my father is doing."

"Oh, so you don't have any contact with him?" Mark asked, not knowing that this was a very difficult topic with Jenny.

"Why should I?" she said. "He ran away with another woman when I was five, and he's never asked about me ever since!"

"Sounds tricky," Mark agreed. "But, well, he's still your father. And you don't *really* know how he feels about everything. If I were you, I would try to contact him."

Jenny's mood suddenly changed.

"What do *you* know?" she shouted angrily. "It's easy for you to say! I'm sure you have a big family, like everyone in

Ireland! Can you actually imagine what it means to be left by your father?"

Mark went quiet and looked at Jenny. There was a long, awkward silence. Finally, after what seemed like hours, Mark spoke. Slowly and clearly.

"Actually, the reason why I'm here in London is that my father and my brother died in a car accident in Cork about four months ago. My mother couldn't stand being in the house on her own any more, so my uncle found her a job here. So, to answer your question: Yes! I do know now what it means to be without a father."

Jenny felt shocked and ashamed of herself. How stupid had she just been!

"I'm so sorry, Mark," Jenny whispered, and her eyes filled with tears.

"No need to feel sorry," Mark said, trying to keep his emotions under control. "It's me who has to deal with that. Sport helps me a lot. Swimming, cycling, running. I'm trying to work it all off. So, my advice was meant seriously: I would try to talk to your father before it's too late. I wish I could still talk to *my* dad."

Jenny did not know what to say. She was still feeling confused and ashamed. Finally, she decided to be completely honest with Mark. She apologized again and told him about her difficult situation. That someone had managed to break into her *Network* website and had made fun of her. And that she had the feeling that a man was following her, which was making her more and more nervous.

"Looks like you've got a real problem then," Mark finally said. "I'm not sure if I can help you, but if you think I can, just let me know."

Back home, Jenny was thinking about the afternoon. Mark's story was still on her mind, and even though she did not know much more about Maths, she had the feeling that she had learnt something important today.

Suddenly, her mobile phone beeped. It was a text message from an unknown number. Jenny could not believe her eyes when she read it.

"Hi Jenny! We should talk. I'm waiting outside. CU James."

Jenny was shaking. She slowly moved towards the window, carefully trying to get a view of the street. There he was! And as if Mr Brunt had been expecting her at the window, he started to wave to Jenny.

Jenny quickly pulled the curtains and got away from the window. So he knew where she lived! And he had her mobile number! How did he do that? And how could she find out what was going on here?

Then she had an idea. Why had she not thought of it earlier? She switched on the computer, opened the search engine and typed in "Mike Armstrong". After about thirty seconds, she was looking at more than 300,000 results, most of which were about an American baseball player and a comedian. Jenny added the word "Tottenham". This time, no results.

Then she tried "James Brunt". Now there were only 50,000 results. She added the word "photographer". Yes! There were several links now, which was enough proof that a photographer called James Brunt did at least exist!

She clicked on the first one and soon found herself on James Brunt's website, a professional photographer from North London. There was even a picture of him, but it was not the James Brunt who kept following her!

Jenny still did not want to give up the idea that at least parts of the story were true. Perhaps Mike was not well-known enough to be on the internet? Then she had another idea. She still had the picture of Mike that she had downloaded when she first visited his profile.

The picture's file name was a long row of numbers and letters. She copied it into the search engine and there it was. The same picture was online. The only difference: the website it was on clearly said that the person was someone called Eddie Wright, a male model from Cheltenham.

Jenny took a deep breath. Now it was a fact. Mike did not exist, and the man who claimed to be James Brunt was definitely someone else!

It was four o'clock. The bell rang, and Kevin's mother opened the door.

"Oh, hello!" she said to Jenny and Vicky. "Come in! You've been here before, haven't you?"

"Yes, I have," Vicky said. "By the way, this is my friend, Jenny."

"Oh, how nice to meet you!" Kevin's mother said, smiling. "Kevin's in his room. You know where it is, don't you?"

"Yes, I do. Thanks," Vicky said, and the two of them went upstairs.

"Kevin!" his mother shouted. "There are two really nice girls here for you. I'll send them up!"

"Two?" Kevin thought and turned around. Before he could switch off his computer or do anything else, Jenny and Vicky had entered his room. Kevin's face went white.

"Hi … er … Jenny. I wasn't … expecting you!"

"I can imagine," Jenny replied coolly. "Like I wasn't expecting what happened to my *Network* profile."

Kevin's face went even more white. He opened his mouth but did not manage to say a word.

"Kevin, be honest," Vicky said in a serious tone. "Did you play around with Jenny's *Network* profile?"

"Er … what … I mean, no … not really … er …"

Jenny looked at his computer screen and saw an image editing program on the lower menu bar.

"May I?" Jenny said to Kevin, and without waiting for a reply, she grabbed the mouse and opened the program. Kevin did not move.

Jenny looked at the upper menu bar and clicked on the 'file' button. The drop-down menu opened, showing a list of recently opened files at the bottom. And there it was: two files that had the names 'jenny1' and 'jenny2'. Jenny clicked on 'jenny1', and the picture of the fat lady on the beach opened. Jenny turned to Kevin.

"Are you sure you have nothing to do with any weird pictures on my profile?" she asked sarcastically.

Now Kevin's face turned bright red.

"Kevin, how could you?" Vicky asked angrily.

"I … er … I didn't," Kevin stammered, but then he finally decided to tell the whole truth. "It … it was only a practical joke. I mean, I didn't want to be mean or anything! I was just so … kind of … disappointed when you unfriended me that I felt like … doing something."

"Well, you kept that 'something' going on for quite a while, didn't you?" Jenny said, and Vicky was surprised how calm she stayed. "Have you got any idea about the damage you've caused?"

"Why?" Kevin replied as if he did not understand. "It was only a few comments, and just on your profile, not on your friends' profiles. I'm sure that after the picture everyone realized that it was just a joke."

"Except for the people who didn't," Vicky said. "It'll be difficult to convince everyone it was you, not Jenny."

"Oh, please don't mention my name," Kevin said nervously. "I'm so sorry! Honestly, I didn't mean to do any harm! It was bad, I know, and I promise I won't ever do it again!"

"But hang on," Jenny suddenly said. "How did you actually find out my password?"

"Oh," Kevin said. "I thought you knew that. Vicky told me."

"What?!" Jenny almost shouted. She did not want to believe what she had just heard. She looked at Vicky, and this time her face turned red.

"Wait a minute," Vicky stammered. "It's not like you think. It kind of … happened by accident."

"Yeah, that's true," Kevin said in defence of Vicky. "I guess that she didn't even realize. When I tried to fix her laptop, she told me her password, 'jenny123'. I was surprised, and she explained that you had each other's names for password because you were best friends. So yours, 'vicky123', was not really difficult to guess."

"I was hoping that he had forgotten about it," Vicky said to Jenny, still feeling ashamed.

"A lot of people use easy passwords, never change them or tell them to other people," Kevin explained. "Or they only use one password for everything."

"And can't you also just hack into someone else's computer?" Vicky asked, still trying to play down her accident.

"Well, that's not as easy as they sometimes show in those cheap Hollywood movies, but it is possible. Spy programs that can search for passwords are much more dangerous because a lot of people still don't use a firewall or even a virus scanner."

"A firewall?" Jenny said as if she did not understand.

"Are you saying you don't have any?" Vicky said, trying to sound particularly surprised. "That could be the reason why your computer is so slow."

"All right, all right," Jenny muttered with her eyes closed. She turned back to Kevin. "But what was this false identity all about? Why did you invent someone called Mike Armstrong?"

Kevin looked confused. "Mike Armstrong? False identity? What are you talking about?"

Jenny and Vicky told Kevin the whole story about Mike, his profile, the chat, the meeting with Mr Brunt and that he seems to be following Jenny.

"Well," Kevin said, "I've got nothing to do with that. This time it looks as if you just weren't careful enough. This Mr Brunt, or whatever his name is, seems to have used a false identity, Mike, to get access to your *Network* profile. And you did him that favour because you accepted him as a friend. I know from your private settings that all your *Network* friends are allowed to see everything. All your messages, comments, pictures, and your private data. That includes your date of birth, your address, and which school you go to. Anything you filled in. And I remember that you even filled in your mobile phone number."

Jenny was shocked. She had never thought that there was any real danger in what she had been doing on *The Network*.

"It might help if we could find out his real identity," Vicky suddenly said. "Can't we identify his IP address?"

Jenny was surprised how much Vicky seemed to know about IT things, but Kevin only smiled.

"*The Network* won't give you that information," he said. "And even if they did, the guy could have used an internet café or something."

"What about his mobile phone number?" Jenny said. "I have it because he keeps sending me text messages!"

"You can try," Kevin said. "But again, a mobile phone company won't give away any data. And if he's clever, he's probably using a pay-as-you-go phone, anyway."

"So you mean we can't find out who he really is?" Jenny asked. "I'm getting more and more scared of him! Do you think he could be dangerous?"

"Don't know," Kevin replied. "But a lot of weird people use the internet for strange purposes. Some of these people are harmless, some are more serious."

"Before we find *that* out, we should get some serious help," Vicky said energetically. "Let's go to the police!"

Vicky and Jenny entered the main police station on High Road, which was just opposite their school. There were a few shabby-looking people waiting in the entrance hall. Vicky asked the assistant behind the desk to speak to someone from the police, and she was told to sit down and wait.

After about half an hour, they were finally allowed into one of the offices. A chubby male police officer in his late fifties was sitting behind a desk, smiling at the two. In the back of the office there was a young female officer typing something on her computer. Jenny and Vicky sat down in front of male officer's desk.

"Now, what can we do for you, young ladies?" he asked in a friendly tone.

"Someone keeps following my friend," Vicky started nervously. "He calls himself Mr Brunt, but he isn't!"

"Yes!" Jenny added. "He got onto *The Network* and found out where I live."

"That's right!" Vicky continued. "And he says he's a photographer, but he isn't!"

WOOD GREEN
POLICE
BOLICE

"And he's got my mobile phone number!" Jenny said. "I've bumped into him three times already, and he always smiles and waves at me! He wants to do a photo shoot, but I don't want that!"

"Wait a minute, wait a minute," the police officer said slowly. He seemed to be strangely unexcited about the whole thing. "Right. Once more. Did this man attack or sexually harass you in any way?"

The two girls looked at each other. "No," Jenny finally said. "At least not yet. But I'm so afraid he's going to! You've got to send someone around to tell him to leave me alone!"

The police officer started smiling again. "I'm afraid we can't do that. If this man hasn't done you any harm, there's not much we can do."

"You mean he has to attack me first before you can do anything?" Jenny asked sarcastically.

"In a way ... yes," he said slowly.

"That's stupid!" Jenny shouted.

"Listen, young lady. This is Wood Green. This is where some of the worst riots in British history started in 2011. We usually deal with thieves, drug addicts, rapists and murderers here. And the government has just cut our budget again. We hardly have enough staff for our regular business. Now, I hope you understand that we cannot have a police officer investigate the case of a man who waves and smiles at a young lady."

"But what are we supposed to do now?" Vicky asked.

Suddenly, the other police officer got up and walked over to them.

"Gordon, I forgot to tell you that Mitch asked for your help some ten minutes ago," she said. "If you want I can deal with this."

The chubby police officer sighed, nodded and walked slowly out of the room. The female officer sat down and smiled at Jenny and Vicky.

"Hi," she said. "I'm Christina Newton. Please excuse my colleague. You know, things are a bit tough at the moment, and he's had very little sleep recently. Now, I've only heard a few bits of your story, so can you tell me again what exactly has happened?"

Jenny and Vicky told Ms Newton all the details while she was listening carefully, nodding from time to time. When they had finished, she took a deep breath and looked at the two.

"Well, I'm afraid at this point there really isn't much we can do. You don't know who that man is or where he lives. What he has done so far is not enough to justify any investigation from our side, and we certainly can't follow you all day just in case he turns up again. But I can understand you're worried. You never know how serious this may become. So, if I were you, I would be even more careful now. Don't reply to his messages. Try not to go anywhere alone. Tell your friends, or perhaps a teacher that you trust. What about your parents? Do they know?"

"I've only got a mum," Jenny replied. "And I don't think it would be a good idea to tell her."

"I see," Ms Newton said. She looked at Jenny, who was now looking a lot less self-confident than she had when she was talking to the other officer.

"I'll tell you what," she finally said. "I'll give you my mobile phone number. If that man turns up again, call me immediately. I can try to send you a colleague if they happen to be nearby. Perhaps we can at least find out his real identity."

The following day, Jenny, Vicky and Mark were talking after school about the events of the past 24 hours. It was still exceptionally hot for this time of year, and in addition, the air was getting more and more humid.

"Ms Newton was really nice," Jenny said. "But I'm a bit worried about what she said. You know, that all this may become more serious. Perhaps the guy is really dangerous!"

"Come on, Jenny," said Vicky, trying to cheer her up. "I'm sure he's not a murderer. Look, at least Emily was listening to me when I tried to explain to her what had happened to your *Network* profile. But I think she needs a bit more time."

"So you've solved the problem of the false messages, but you still don't know who that man is who keeps stalking you?" Mark asked.

"Exactly," Jenny and Vicky replied almost together.

"Have you told your mum about it?" Mark asked.

"No way!" Jenny said, looking almost shocked. "My mum would freak out if she knew that a man was following me. Especially if she knew that he got in contact with me through *The Network*."

"It must be a hard time for you at the moment," Vicky said.

"Well, I must admit that I'm getting more and more nervous," Jenny agreed. "I couldn't really sleep last night, and I can't concentrate in class. Just this morning I had the feeling again that he was following me on my way to school."

"I can fully understand that," Vicky tried to comfort her. She could see that, despite Jenny's tough nature, she was now close to tears.

"You know, I'm beginning to see a Mr Brunt behind every bush," Jenny said quietly.

"And there's nothing you or we can do?" Mark asked.

"Well, Ms Newton said I should try not go anywhere alone ... so could you do me a favour and walk me home?" Jenny stammered.

"No worries!" Mark said and smiled at her.

Jenny felt safe and relaxed while she was walking home with Mark. He told her a bit about Ireland, Cork and his family, and she managed to forget about her problems with the stalker. Soon they arrived at Jenny's house.

"Right, I've gotta go now and get my swimming things," Mark said.

Jenny felt strange. Somehow she did not want to let Mark go now.

"Perhaps I could come along to the pool again some time?" Jenny asked shyly. "It'd be great if you could keep teaching me. That means, if you don't think I'm a hopeless case."

"Sure, no problem," Mark replied. "We'll definitely do that. See you at school tomorrow."

"Yeah, see ya." She watched Mark until he had disappeared around the corner. When she turned around, she got the shock of her life.

"Hello Jenny," Mr Brunt said. "How are you?"

Where did he come from? Had he been hiding behind one of the trees? How did he always manage to just appear out of nowhere?

"Now, Jenny, I can't understand why you don't want to grab this chance of your life," Mr Brunt said quietly, staring at her. "So many girls dream of being discovered. We have loads of applicants every day. But it's your face that we've been looking for. Just imagine, your pictures would appear in all the trendy fashion magazines. All your friends would be really jealous of you!"

Jenny was also staring at him but could neither move nor speak. Her eyes felt strangely out of focus, and it became more and more difficult to listen to him.

"So why don't you just come along and we'll talk about it again," he said, getting closer to Jenny.

Jenny showed no reaction, but then her eyes refocused. Someone had approached Mr Brunt from behind and was now standing about two metres away from him. Her eyes and mouth opened up wide.

"Excuse me, sir," Mark said. "I'm not sure she really wants to talk to you."

Mr Brunt slowly turned around and smiled at Mark. "Well, we're actually having a nice chat, so I would say it's none of your business, young man, is it?"

The next thing happened quite fast. Mark suddenly went up to Mr Brunt, getting very close to his face. Staring into his eyes, he spoke slowly but in a tone that Jenny had never heard or expected from him.

"Listen, you dirty old git, if you keep stalking my girlfriend, I'll get all my mates from the *Shannon Arms* and we'll teach you a lesson, I swear!"

ST THOMAS

Mark's behaviour seemed to have had an effect. Mr Brunt was taken aback, looking confused. So was Jenny, partly because of Mark's unexpected move and partly because of his use of the word 'girlfriend' for her. But soon the moment of surprise had faded away, and Mr Brunt took a step back.

"You will regret this, young man!" he shouted at Mark.

"Shut up and get the hell out of here!" Mark shouted back at him, and once again this seemed to impress Mr Brunt. He took some further steps back, then turned around and started to walk away quickly. Mark looked at Jenny for a few seconds.

"Stay with me" Jenny whispered, but Mark decided to follow him. When he got to the corner of Queen's Road, Mark saw Mr Brunt get into a car and drive off before he could reach him.

Jenny was still upset. She could not move. Her body was shaking all over from what she had just witnessed. Her mind was empty, and her feelings were a strange mix of shock, fear, confusion and even pride at what Mark had just done for her. She kept staring at the corner behind which the two of them had disappeared when she suddenly saw Mark running towards her.

"Pen and paper, quick!" he panted. Jenny reached into her bag and, after a hectic search, found a pencil and a piece of paper.

"Write down!" Mark said out of breath and he closed his eyes. "LM … 60 … SMR."

"What's that?" Jenny asked, still looking confused.

"Black Ford Focus! His car! We've got him!"

Jenny was in her room with Mark. She had switched on her computer and, as usual, was waiting for it to finish booting up. Perhaps Kevin could have a look at it some time?

"So you think this is going to work?" Jenny asked, looking a bit sceptical.

"At least it's worth trying," Mark replied as he typed the registration number into the search engine. He pressed 'Enter', and a small circle on the screen showed that there was at least some activity going on inside Jenny's computer.

"This … bloody … com … puter!" Jenny muttered, but then she looked at Mark. "Sorry about that," she quickly said.

There were no results. He added 'number plate' and other key words, but again there was nothing.

"Oh well," Mark said. "Never mind. It would have surprised me if the DVLA kept an online database that anybody can access."

"The DVLA?" Jenny asked.

"That's the Driver and Vehicle Licensing Agency. They register all the number plates in Britain. The only other thing we can try is phone them up to find out the owner of the car."

They found a phone number on the internet. Mark decided to make the phone call. They knew they needed a good story but could not think of anything fantastic. Still, Mark was having a go.

"Hello," Mark said when he had finally got through to the right person." My name's Dave Allen. I need to find the owner of a black Ford Focus. The registration number is LM 60 SMR."

"I'm sorry, but we're not allowed to give out any information like that," the other person said.

"I can imagine," Mark continued, "but I have just accidentally scratched that person's car, and I would like to get in touch with him or her."

"Well, why don't you leave your number at the car so they can phone you?" the suggestion was.

"Er … did I just say I scratched it?" Mark tried to change his strategy. "Sorry, must be the heat. Of course, they scratched *my* car."

"Well, in that case you had better go to the police, anyway, if you want to make any claims. They can also find out the owner through their information system."

"Really?" Mark said, sounding a bit disappointed. "All right then. Thanks very much. Bye."

Jenny had listened to the conversation and could see that it had not been successful.

"No chance," Mark said. "We would have to go to the police. They seem to be the only ones allowed to access the database."

"Of course!" Jenny suddenly shouted. "I completely forgot. How stupid of me!"

She took out her mobile phone and started to type a text message: *Dear Ms Newton, …*

The weekend passed strangely quietly. Mr Brunt had stopped appearing out of the blue, but Jenny was still a bit sceptical. Had Mark really scared him enough so that he would finally leave her alone? She did not quite want to believe it, but she felt a bit more relaxed after what he had done.

She met up with Mark on Saturday to catch up with Maths, and they went for an ice cream afterwards. It was another hot day, and Jenny hung out with Mark almost the whole day, which made her completely forget about the text message she had sent to Ms Newton. She did not even wonder why Ms Newton had not replied yet.

Now it was Sunday afternoon, and Jenny was on her way to meet up with Vicky at *Stardust's*. It was still very hot, but the sky was beginning to get more and more cloudy. She had just turned into High Road when her mobile phone beeped. She looked at it, and her good mood changed immediately. It was a message from Mr Brunt!

"Hello Jenny! Hope your friend wasn't too jealous that you will be a success! Talk to you later."

"This guy is a real pain in the neck!" Jenny said to herself. She could feel all the stress rising inside her again, and she was glad that she was about to see Vicky.

"Hi Jenny!" Vicky said when she saw her. "Good news! I've managed to convince H&M to stop sulking and talk to you again. And Paul Bennington said it wasn't a big deal, either."

"Thank you so much, Vicky," Jenny said. "You're a real friend. I've just had some bad news. Mr Brunt has sent another text."

At that moment, her mobile phone beeped again. Jenny rolled her eyes, but this time it was a message from Ms Newton: *Dear Jenny, We've got the identity. Could you come and see me at the police station? I'm there all afternoon. Best, Christina.*

Jenny quickly began to write a reply: *Thanks! I'll be there asap.*

Vicky was puzzled. "Have you started replying to him now?"

"No," Jenny explained. "It was Ms Newton. She seems to have found out Mr Brunt's real identity!"

Half an hour later, Jenny and Vicky were sitting in Ms Newton's office.

"Sorry for my late reply," Ms Newton said. "I hope that man hasn't been causing any further trouble since."

"Not really," Jenny said. "It was pretty quiet at the weekend, but just an hour ago he sent me another text message."

"Right. Well, I've managed to find out the owner of that car," she announced. "And I've done some more research for you on the internet. Now, first I'd like you to tell me if this is the man who keeps following you."

She turned her computer screen so that Jenny and Vicky could see it from where they were sitting.

"That's him!" Jenny shouted. "Definitely!"

"Good. So his name is Peter Thorne, and he lives at 23 Boreham Road," Ms Newton went on. "He's an insurance salesman who works in the Wood Green area. He often visits people at home and these things."

"That would explain why he always seems to be everywhere!" Jenny concluded.

"Oh, and another interesting piece of information: he's got a wife and a young kid. That would perhaps explain why things went a bit quiet for you at the weekend."

Jenny and Vicky looked at each other. They knew a lot about the internet, of course, but for a moment they were both reminded how easy it sometimes was to find out about people.

"What do you suggest we should do now?" Jenny finally said.

"Well, as he still seems to be bothering you, we should perhaps pay him a visit and ask him a few questions," Ms Newton said, smiling. "But I suggest we go and see him at his workplace, not at home. I wouldn't like to cause any unnecessary trouble for his wife."

It was Monday afternoon. The weather had finally changed. The whole morning had seen some serious thunderstorms, and now it was still raining heavily.

Ms Newton had arranged with Jenny to pick her up after school. She had asked for an appointment with Mr Thorne by e-mail, pretending to be very interested in taking out an insurance policy, and, to her surprise, had got a positive reply immediately. Now Jenny and Ms Newton, who was wearing plain clothes instead of her uniform, were driving to the insurance office.

At the office they were welcomed by Mr Thorne's secretary, who led them to his room. When Jenny and Ms Newton entered the room, Mr Thorne got up from his desk and quickly walked towards them, ready to shake their hands. He looked at Jenny and stopped. It was as if someone had pushed the pause button on a DVD-player. Mr Thorne did not move or speak. He just stood there like a statue, and his face went white. But then he pulled himself together and went on to shake Ms Newton's hand.

"Hello Ms Newton," he said, trying to sound as normal as possible. "I'm sorry, but I had just remembered something very important. Anyway, and this is your daughter, I suppose?" He looked at Jenny.

"Hello Mr Thorne," Ms Newton said. "No, this is not my daughter but a girl that has come to seek help with us. I work for the Metropolitan Police." She quickly showed a police badge. "Jenny says that you've been stalking her for the past two weeks."

"Me?" Mr Thorne said, looking surprised. "Dear me, no. Why should I? I'm sure this must be some misunderstanding."

"Of course you have!" Jenny shouted. "You pretended to be some Mr Brunt, who wanted to do a photo shoot with me! I've told you several times to leave me alone, but you won't!"

"My dear young lady," Mr Thorne said to Jenny, "I don't know you. You should be more careful with what you say."

"Well," Ms Newton interrupted, "we have reasons to believe that what Jenny says is true. Another witness saw you in front of Jenny's home. In fact, he says that he had to help Jenny to keep you away from her."

Mr Thorne was listening with an empty expression on his face when suddenly a phone was ringing from somewhere.

"He also said that he saw you drive off in a black Focus car. This is how we found out about you. What do you say about this?"

Mr Thorne was still staring at her absent-mindedly while the ringing became louder.

"Excuse me for a second," he suddenly said and turned around. He reached into his pocket and took out his mobile phone. "Hello?"

"Hello Mr Thorne," Jenny said. "Or shall I say, Mr Brunt?"

Mr Thorne turned around quickly to see that Jenny was talking to him on her mobile phone. He slowly lowered his hand and switched off his own phone.

"I just called the number that all those text messages came from," Jenny said. "And hey, it's yours!"

"Now," Ms Newton said, "Mr Thorne, I have to tell you that what you've been doing can be seen as a criminal offence. I understand that you have a wife and a child, and you seem to have a responsible job, so I suppose you might be interested in not making your activities public."

Mr Thorne nodded slowly.

"So I suggest you see this as a last warning. You will stop following or bothering Jenny, and if I were you I would not even think of doing the same thing again with other girls. We have your name and address. I believe you don't want to cause any further trouble for yourself. Do you think we can agree on that?"

"Promised," he said through his teeth.

They left Mr Thorne's office, and Jenny felt like a huge load had been taken off her shoulder.

CHAPTER NINE A fresh start

It had been raining almost the whole week, and temperatures had gone down. It felt like autumn had finally arrived. The trees had become more colourful, and the air was fresh.

Jenny was waiting in the schoolyard for Vicky. She smiled when she read Vicky's usual text message that she was going to be late. No worries. Everything just felt so much better than a week ago.

While she was waiting, Haylie and Emily arrived. They stopped to have a quick chat with Jenny, had a laugh together and then went on. The whole story about *The Network* seemed to be forgotten. In fact, Jenny's relationship with the two girls even seemed to have improved.

"Hi Jenny! How are you?" Vicky smiled when she arrived.

"Fine, thanks," Jenny replied.

"It shows," Vicky said. "You look so much better than last week."

"Yeah," Jenny admitted. "I'm so glad it's all over. Ms Newton was ever so nice. I was talking to her again, and she said I was lucky that Mr Thorne wasn't a typical stalker. She had some pretty scary stories to tell! Oh, by the way, I decided to tell my mum about what happened."

Vicky looked surprised. "What did she say?"

"It was actually OK," Jenny said. "I was worried because you know how much she hates *The Network*. I thought she'd blame me. But she seemed pretty happy I'd told her."

"That's great news," Vicky replied. "Maybe you should get into trouble more often."

Jenny laughed. "No thanks! But the whole thing's even kind of brought us a bit closer together – strangely! We had a long talk the other day, and I had the feeling that for the first time she was actually listening to what I was saying. She also told me a lot about my father. I asked her if she would mind if I contacted him, and she said no, so I did."

"Really? So you've been talking to your father?" Vicky asked.

"Yes! I phoned him yesterday. He lives in Darlington, up in the North."

"Darlington? I've been there. It's a very nice place," Vicky commented.

"Anyway, he was really happy to talk to me. I couldn't believe it! It looks like he always thought that I didn't want any contact with him. Which is kind of half-true, of course. But anyway, now we're going to meet up. He's coming down to London next week! Who knows – this might be a fresh start?"

"Yeah, who knows," Vicky smiled at Jenny. "By the way, will you keep using *The Network*, after all the trouble you've had?"

"Definitely!" replied Jenny quickly. "But I've been cleaning up my profile. I have deleted a lot of information about myself, changed my private settings and unfriended everybody I've never met in reality. My list of friends is now down to 53!"

"53?!" Vicky said, surprised. "Well I hope you haven't deleted me!"

"Don't worry, I would never delete you!"

It was ten to four. Jenny was in her room. She was glad that her Maths test had been OK, thanks to Mark's help.

Now they had arranged to meet up. It was four o'clock, and Jenny noticed that she felt a bit excited.

The door bell rang. Mark was as reliable as a real friend could ever be.

Vocabulary

Abbreviations
sb. = somebody;
sth. = something;
jdm. = jemandem;
jdn. = jemanden;
ugs. = umgangsprachlich

A

absent-minded ['æbsənt 'maɪndɪd] geistesabwesend
(to) **accept** [ək'sept]: **to accept a friend** jdn. als Freund/in bestätigen
access ['ækses] Zugang
accidentally [ˌæksɪ'dentəli] versehentlich
account [ə'kaʊnt] Konto
addictive [ə'dɪktɪv] suchterzeugend
(to) **admit** [əd'mɪt] zugeben
amusing [ə'mjuːzɪŋ] amüsant
apprehensive [ˌæprɪ'hensɪv] besorgt
(to) **approach sb.** [ə'prəʊtʃ] jdm. näher kommen
architecture ['ɑːkɪtektʃə] Architektur
(to) **arrange** [ə'reɪndʒ] planen
arrogance ['ærəgəns] Arroganz
asap [ˌeɪeseɪ'piː]: **as soon as possible** so schnell wie möglich
ashamed [ə'ʃeɪmd]: (to) **be ashamed** sich schämen
(to) **assure** [ə'ʃʊə] versichern
automatically [ˌɔːtə'mætɪkli] automatisch
awkward ['ɔːkwəd] peinlich; unangenehm

B

(to) **backtrack** ['bæktræk] einen Rückzieher machen
basically ['beɪsɪkli] eigentlich
beep [biːp] Piep
(to) **bend** [bend] sich vorbeugen
bitch *(vulgär)* [bɪtʃ] Schlampe
blank [blæŋk] leer
bloody *(vulgär)* ['blʌdi] verdammt
(to) **boot up** [buːt] *(einen Computer)* hochfahren
(to) **bother sb.** ['bɒðə] jdn. stören
boyfriend ['bɔɪfrend] Freund
brain [breɪn] Gehirn
brainless ['breɪnləs] hirnlos
breaststroke ['brestˌstrəʊk] Bruststil
breath [breθ]: (to) **take a deep breath** tief einatmen

(to) **brighten up** [ˌbraɪtn'ʌp] aufheitern
broad [brɔːd] breit
brochure ['brəʊʃə] Broschüre
brownie points ['braʊni pɔɪnts] Pluspunkte
btw: by the way übrigens
bubble ['bʌbl] Blase
(to) **burst** [bɜːst] platzen
businessman ['bɪznəsmən] Geschäftsmann
button ['bʌtn] Taste

C

Catholic ['kæθlɪk] katholisch
certainly ['sɜːtnli] bestimmt
(to) **chat sb. up** [ˌtʃæt'ʌp] jdn. anmachen
cheek [tʃiːk] Wange
chilly ['tʃɪli] kühl
choice [tʃɔɪs] Wahl
chubby ['tʃʌbi] pummelig
chunk [tʃʌŋk] Stück
claim [kleɪm]: (to) **make claims** Ansprüche erheben
colleague ['kɒliːg] Kollege/Kollegin
comedian [kə'miːdiən] Komiker/in
(to) **comment** ['kɒment] kommentieren
(to) **concentrate** ['kɒnsntreɪt] sich konzentrieren
(to) **contain** [kən'teɪn] enthalten
(to) **convince** [kən'vɪns] überzeugen
convincing [kən'vɪnsɪŋ] überzeugend
corridor ['kɒrɪdɔː] Korridor
counterpart ['kaʊntəpɑːt] Gegenstück
criminal offence ['krɪmɪnl 'əfens] Straftat
CU: See you! Bis bald!
curtains ['kɜːtnz] Vorhänge
cute [kjuːt] süß, hübsch

D

damage ['dæmɪdʒ] schaden
(to) **dare** [deə] wagen, sich trauen
data ['deɪtə] Daten
database ['deɪtəbeɪs] Datenbank
(to) **de-activate** [ˌdiː'æktɪveɪt] stilllegen *(ein Konto)*
deal [diːl]: **no big deal** kein Ding
(to) **delete** [dɪ'liːt] löschen
dialogue ['daɪəlɒg] Dialog
direction [də'rekʃn] Richtung
(to) **disturb** [dɪ'stɜːb] stören
drug addict [ˌdrʌg'ædɪkt] Drogenabhängiger
dunno *(ugs.)* [də'nəʊ]: **I don't know.** Ich weiß es nicht.

E

emotions [ɪ'məʊʃnz] Emotionen, Gefühle
energetically [ˌenə'dʒetɪkli] energisch
enjoyable [ɪn'dʒɔɪəbl] amüsant
entrance ['entrəns] Eingang
(to) **examine** [ɪg'zæmɪn] untersuchen

exceptionally [ɪk'sepʃənəli] außergewöhnlich
eye-contact ['aɪ kɒntækt] Augenkontakt

F

(to) **fade** [feɪd] verschwinden
faint smile [feɪnt smaɪl] angedeutetes Lächeln
false [fɔːls] falsch
familiar [fə'mɪliə] bekannt
(to) **fancy sb.** ['fænsi] jdn. gut finden
fashionable ['fæʃnəbl] modisch
firewall ['faɪəwɔːl] *Schutzprogramm für Computer*
firm [fɜːm] Firma
first thing ['fɜːst θɪŋ] als Erstes
firstly ['fɜːstli] erstens
(to) **fix** [fɪks] reparieren
(to) **flick through** [flɪk θru] durchblättern
folder ['fəʊldə] Ordner
follow-up ['fɒləʊʌp] nachfolgend
For God's sake! [fə 'gɒdz seɪk] Um Gottes Willen!
forties ['fɔːtiz]: **a man in his forties** ein Mann in den Vierzigern
forward ['fɔːwəd] *hier:* direkt
fresh [freʃ] frisch
front crawl [frʌnt krɔːl] Kraulschwimmen
frustrated [frʌ'streɪtɪd] frustriert
fun [fʌn]: (to) **make fun of sth.** sich über etwas lustig machen
further ['fɜːðə] weiter

G

GCSE [ˌdʒiːsiːes'iː] **General Certificate of Secondary Education** *(Schulabschluss im britischen Schulsystem)*
(to) **giggle** ['gɪgl] kichern
ginger ['dʒɪndʒə] rot (Haare)
git *(vulgär)* [gɪt] *Abwertender Begriff für einen Mann*
goggles ['gɒglz] Schutzbrille
gotta *(ugs.)* ['gɒtə]: **(I've) got to** (Ich) muss
(to) **grin** [grɪn] grinsen
(to) **groan** [grəʊn] stöhnen

H

(to) **hack into** [hæk] *(in ein Konto)* eindringen
haircut ['heəkʌt] Haarschnitt
handful ['hændfʊl] Hand voll
hardly ['hɑːdli] kaum
(to) **harm** [hɑːm] schaden
harm [hɑːm]: **can't do any harm** kann nicht schaden
heavily ['hevili] tief
hectic ['hektɪk] hektisch
hell [hel]: **Get the hell out of here!** *(vulgär)* Hau ab!
high definition [haɪ ˌdefɪ'nɪʃn] hochauflösend
holiday resort ['hɒlədeɪ rɪˌzɔːt] Ferienanlage

I

icon ['aɪkɒn] Symbol
(to) **ignore** [ɪg'nɔː] ignorieren
immediate [ɪ'miːdiət] sofort

in addition [ə'dɪʃn] zusätzlich
inbox ['ɪnbɒks] Posteingang
(to) **insult sb.** [ɪn'sʌlt] jdn. beleidigen
insurance policy [ɪn'ʃʊərəns 'pɒləsi] Versicherungspolice
insurance salesman [ɪn'ʃʊərəns seɪlzmən] Versicherungskaufmann
(to) **investigate** [ɪn'vestɪgeɪt] untersuchen
IP address [aɪːpi ə'dres] IP-Adresse
irritated ['ɪrɪteɪtɪd] irritiert

K

keyboard ['kiːbɔːd] Tastatur

L

label ['leɪbl] Bezeichnung
Laters! *(ugs.)* ['leɪ.təs]: **See you later!** Bis später!
(to) **lean** [liːn] lehnen
left-hand ['lefthænd]auf der linken Seite
length [leŋθ] *hier:* Bahn *(im Schwimmbad)*
lifetime ['laɪftaɪm] Lebenszeit
(to) **log off** [ˌlɒg'ɒf] abmelden, ausloggen
(to) **log on/in** [ˌlɒg'ɒn/ˌlɒg'ɪn] einloggen
lol: laughing out load laut lachend
lower; (to) **lower** ['ləʊə] niedriger, tiefer; senken

M

mags: magazines [mægz] Zeitschriften
(to) **manipulate** [mə'nɪpjuleɪt] manipulieren
manners ['mænəz] Manieren
meaningful ['miːnɪŋfl] *hier:* aussagekräftig
meantime ['miːntaɪm] Zwischenzeit
(to) **mention** ['menʃn] erwähnen
misunderstanding [ˌmɪsʌndə'stændɪŋ] Missverständnis
(to) **mutter** ['mʌtə] murmeln
mutual ['mjuːtʃuəl] gemeinsam

N

neither … nor… ['naɪðə nɔː] weder … noch …
nerd [nɜːd] Computerfreak
nickname ['nɪkneɪm] Spitzname
nightmare ['naɪtmeə] Alptraum
none [nʌn] keine/r
(to) **note** [nəʊt]: **note sth. down** (sich) etwas notieren
number plate ['nʌmbə pleɪt] Nummernschild (Auto)
obvious ['ɒbviəs] offensichtlich
odd [ɒd] seltsam, komisch
openness ['əʊpənnəs] Offenheit
(to) **overlap** [ˌəʊvə'læp] überlappen
overreaction [ˌəʊvəri'ækʃn] Überreaktion

P

Paddy ['pædi] *abwertender Begriff für Iren*
(to) **pant** [pænt] keuchen
partly ['pɑːtli] teilweise
password ['pɑːswɜːd] Passwort, Kennwort
pay-as-you-go mobile phone [ˌpeɪəzju'gəʊ] Prepaid-Handy
peace [piːs]: **leave me in peace** lass mich in Ruhe
pics [pɪks]: **pictures** Bilder
police officer [pə'liːs ɒfɪsə] Polizist/in
(to) **pop up** [ˌpɒp'ʌp] *(im Internet)* plötzlich auftauchen
pop-up message ['pɒpʌp 'mesɪdʒ] Pop-up-Fenster
post [pəʊst]: (to) **post a comment** einen Kommentar eintragen
presence ['prezns] Anwesenheit
(to) **press** [pres] drücken
previous ['priːviəs] vorherige/r
pride [praɪd] Stolz
profession [prə'feʃn] Beruf
properly ['prɒpəli] richtig
puncture ['pʌŋktʃə] Loch
puncture repair kit ['pʌŋktʃə rɪ'peə(r) kɪt] Flickzeug
purpose ['pɜːpəs]: **on purpose** mit Absicht
push [pʊʃ]: (to) **push sb.'s button** jdn. irritieren, jdn. provozieren
pushing and shoving [pʊʃɪŋ ənd ʃʌvɪŋ] Gedrängel

Q

quid *(ugs.)*: **pounds** [kwɪd] Pfund

R

rapist ['reɪpɪst] Vergewaltiger/in
rather ['rɑːðə] ziemlich
refocus [ri'fəʊkəs]: (to) **refocus the eyes** den Blick wieder fokussieren
registration [ˌredʒɪ'streɪʃn] Anwesenheitskontrolle *(wenn man die Klassenliste durchgeht)*
registration number [ˌredʒɪ'streɪʃn nʌmbə] Autokennzeichen
(to) **regret** [rɪ'gret] bereuen
relieved [rɪ'liːvd] erleichtert
(to) **remind** [rɪ'maɪnd] erinnern an
restricted [rɪ'strɪktɪd] eingeschränkt
(to) **return** [rɪ'tɜːn] zurückkkehren
(to) **reveal** [rɪ'viːl] offenbaren
review [rɪ'vjuː] Bericht
rice [raɪs] Reis
ridiculous [rɪ'dɪkjələs] lächerlich
rivalry ['raɪvlri] Konkurrenz
(to) **roll** [rəʊl]: **roll your eyes** die Augen rollen
Rubbish! ['rʌbɪʃ] Quatsch!

S

sarcastic [sɑː'kæstɪk] sarkastisch
sceptical ['skeptɪkl] skeptisch
schoolyard ['skuːljɑːd] Schulhof
(to) **scratch** [skrætʃ] zerkratzen
screen [skriːn] (Bild)schirm
(to) **scroll** [skrəʊl] scrollen
search engine ['sɜːtʃ endʒɪn] Suchmaschine
secretary ['sekrətri] Sekretär/in
sense of humour [sens əv 'hjuːmə] Sinn für Humor
sexually ['seksjʊəli] sexuell
shabby ['ʃæbi] schäbig
shallow end ['ʃæləʊ end] Anfangsbereich/ Nichtschwimmerbereich des Schwimmbads
(a) **shame** [ʃeɪm] schade
sharp [ʃɑːp]: **at 5 o'clock sharp** um punkt 5 Uhr
(to) **shut down** [ˌʃʌt'daʊn] *(einen Computer)* herunterfahren
(to) **sigh** [saɪ] seufzen
silence ['saɪləns] Stille
similar ['sɪmələ] ähnlich
simply ['sɪmpli] einfach
(to) **slide** [slaɪd] rutschen
slim [slɪm] schlank
smooth [smuːð] geschmeidig
(to) **snarl** [snɑːl] knurren
(to) **sneer** [snɪə] grinsen
(to) **sob** [sɒb] schluchzen
solution [sə'luːʃn] Lösung
(to) **squint** [skwɪnt] blinzeln
(to) **stalk** [stɔːk] jdm. nachstellen
stalker ['stɔː.kə] Stalker/in *(eine Person, die jmd. anderen zwanghaft verfolgt und belästigt)*
(to) **stammer** ['stæmə] stottern, stammeln
(to) **step** [step] treten
strategy ['strætədʒi] Strategie
(to) **suggest** [sə'dʒest] vorschlagen
suggestion [sə'dʒestʃən] Vorschlag
suit [suːt] Anzug
(to) **sulk** [sʌlk] schmollen
(to) **swear** [sweə] schwören
(to) **swim laps** [swɪm læpz] Bahnen schwimmen
(to) **switch on/off** [ˌswɪtʃ'ɒn/ ˌswɪtʃ'ɒf] an-/ausschalten

T

taken aback ['teɪkn ə'bæk] schockiert
technical ['teknɪkl] technisch
textbook ['tekstbʊk] Schulbuch, Lehrbuch
thin [θɪn] dünn
(to) **tick** [tɪk] ein Häckchen machen
tiring ['taɪərɪŋ] ermüdend
truth [truːθ] Wahrheit
(to) **type** [taɪp] tippen
type [taɪp]: **not your type of guy** nicht dein Typ

U

underwater [ˌʌndəˈwɔːtə] unter Wasser

unexcited [ˌʌnɪkˈsaɪtɪd] uninteressiert

unfit [ʌnˈfɪt] nicht im Form

(to) **unfriend** [ˌʌnˈfrend] jdn. als Freund/in löschen, „entfreunden“

unlock [ˌʌnˈlɒk] entsperren

unnecessary [ʌnˈnesəsəri] unnötig

(to) **unpack** [ˌʌnˈpæk] auspacken

unusual [ʌnˈjuːʒuəl] ungewöhnlich

(to) **upload** [ʌpˈləʊd] hochladen

V

virus scanner [ˈvaɪrəs skænə] Virenscanner

W

wanna [ˈwʌnə]: **(I) want to** (Ich) will

well-built [ˌwelˈbɪlt] gut gebaut

well-known [ˌwelˈnəʊn] gut bekannt

What a ...! [wɒt ə] Was für ein(e) ...!

What's up? [ˈwɒts ʌp] Was ist los?

wise [waɪz] weise

(to) **witness** [ˈwɪtnəs] bezeugen

Y

yob *(ugs.)* [jɒb] Rüpel

Check your understanding

Chapter 1

1 Why does Jenny accept Kevin as a friend on *The Network*?
2 What does Jenny's mother think about *The Network*?
3 Where does Jenny live?
4 Why does Jenny's mother worry about Jenny?

Chapter 2

1 What does Haylie show Jenny?
2 How did Vicky get to know Kevin?
3 Where does Mark come from?
4 How long has Mark been living in London?

Chapter 3

1 What does Jenny do when she gets home?
2 How does Kevin get in contact with Jenny?
3 Why does Jenny 'unfriend' Kevin?
4 Who is Mike?

Chapter 4

1 Why did Mark manage to do the Maths homework?
2 What is Mark looking for in the area?
3 Why can't Vicky join Mark and Jenny at the pool?
4 What does Mark say about *The Network*?

Chapter 5

1 How does Emily react when Jenny says hello to her?
2 What does Jenny see when she logs on to *The Network*?

3 What does Mike offer Jenny?
4 Who is Mr Brunt?
5 What has happened to Mike's profile?

Chapter 6

1 Why are Anna, Maria and Chris laughing at Jenny?
2 What are Mark and Jenny planning to do in the afternoon?
3 Who does Vicky think is responsible for Jenny's *Network* comments?
4 What happens in the supermarket?
5 Why did Mark move to London?

Chapter 7

1 How did Kevin find out Jenny's password?
2 What information are Jenny's *Network* friends allowed to see?
3 What does Ms Newton give Jenny?
4 What does Mark manage to find out?

Chapter 8

1 How do Mark and Jenny try to find out the owner of the car?
2 Who is Mr Brunt really?
3 What does Ms Newton plan to do?
4 Why does Jenny call Mr Brunt's phone number?

Chapter 9

1 Who is Jenny going to meet next week?
2 Has Jenny fallen in love with Mark?